Carlson's Guide to

Landscape Painting

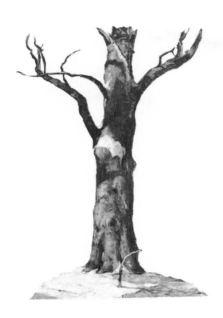

By JOHN F. CARLSON, N.A.

DOVER PUBLICATIONS, INC., NEW YORK

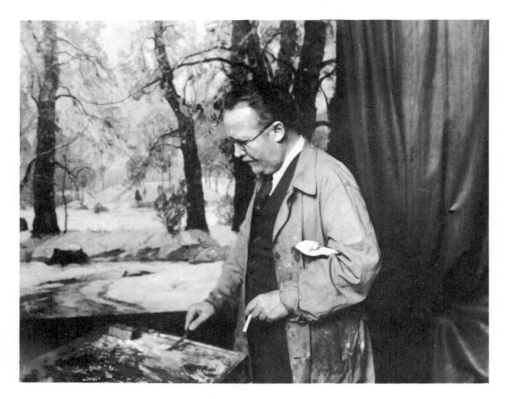

John F. Carlson was elected a member
of the National Academy of Design, the
New York Water Color Club, the American
Water Color Society, the National Arts
Club and the Salmagundi Club. He is rep-
resented in the permanent collections of
the Metropolitan Museum, the Corcoran
Gallery (Washington, D. C.), the Art Insti-
tute of Chicago, the Toledo Museum of
Art, the Butler Art Institute (Youngstown,
Ohio), the Brooks Memorial Gallery
(Memphis, Tenn.), the Baltimore Museum
of Fine Arts, the Fort Worth Art Associa-
tion, and many other collections.

Published in Canada by General Publishing Company, Ltd., 30 Lesmill Road, Don Mills, Toronto,
Ontario.
Published in the United Kingdom by Constable
and Company, Ltd.

This Dover edition, first published in 1973, is an
unabridged and unaltered republication of the revised edition published in 1958. The work is here
reprinted by special arrangement with the previous
publisher, Sterling Publishing Company, Inc., 419
Park Avenue South, New York, N. Y. 10016.

International Standard Book Number: 0-486-22927-0
Library of Congress Catalog Card Number: 72-95436

Manufactured in the United States of America
Dover Publications, Inc.
180 Varick Street
New York, N. Y. 10014

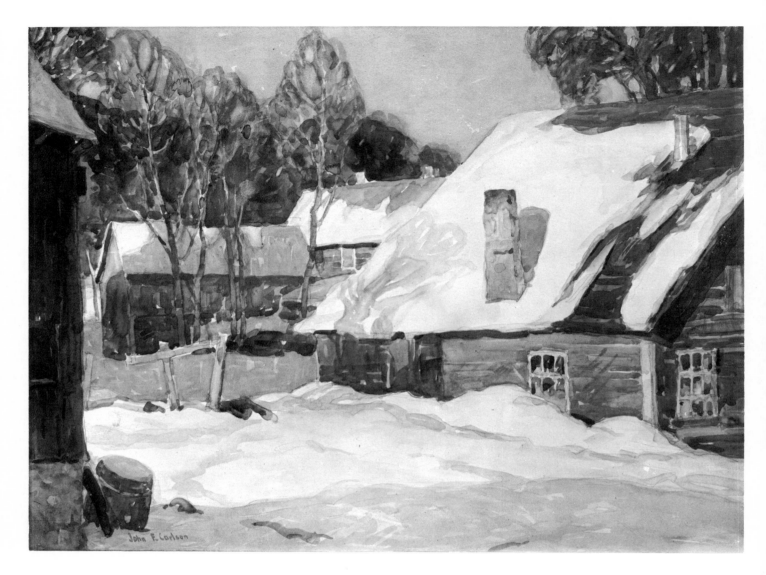

CATSKILL WINTER

TABLE OF CONTENTS

INTRODUCTION

John F. Carlson was an alert boy of nine when he first saw the United States after journeying overseas from his native Sweden. In 1890, he lived in Buffalo. He was fifteen then when he started to paint. Somehow he found time to study at night while working during the day in a lithographic shop where he did drawings on the huge stones then common. He went to classes under Lucius Hitchcock at the Albright Art Gallery.

In 1902 Carlson won the Art Students' League Scholarship and came to New York where he worked with Frank Vincent DuMond at the League School. Carlson read widely, and a broad humanism and classic education became part of him. Music was a great and inspiring force in his life. He brought all of this to bear upon his painting and teaching. In this book, which is *much more* than a compendium of information on how to paint, one can feel the whole dimension of the man: his interests and his closeness to nature.

After six years at the League, he was appointed Assistant to Birge Harrison, Director of the Art Students' League's Summer School at Woodstock. Woodstock country became his own and many of his most famous landscapes were inspired by the hills, woods, and streams of the Catskill countryside.

Carlson succeeded Harrison as Director, and for eight years worked hard at building the Woodstock school into a national institution. During this time many honors were given him for his work as a painter, among them the coveted Carnegie and Altman Prizes.

Carlson went west in 1920 to Colorado Springs, in the Rocky Mountains, where he became co-founder of the Broadmoor Academy. Museums sought his landscapes and they are to be found in the permanent collections of the Metropolitan Museum of Art, the Corcoran Gallery, the Art Institute of Chicago, Toledo Museum, and many others.

He returned to Woodstock in 1922, finding there a never-ending source of subject matter for his landscape art. Excepting two years of teaching with Emil Gruppé at Gloucester, he worked at Woodstock until his untimely death in 1945.

Carlson was critical of the traveling painters who required the "picturesque" to move them to paint. He felt and found in Nature at his back door the changing light and drama of the skies, and from this he made pictures of quality.

Carlson is essentially a "verist," who painted what he saw, transformed by how he felt about it, always recognizing that in nature lay the wellspring. As a teacher he is wider and more liberal in his view. He anticipated the effect of modern ideas in abstraction, though he cared little for non-objective painting.

The "Guide to Landscape Painting" is his only literary work, but it is completely Carlson. Crammed into its pages are the thoughts and experiences of a lifetime of painting and teaching. Undoubtedly it is a good book for the beginner, but the old hand at art will appreciate its honesty and broadness of viewpoint. It confines itself to the mechanics of landscape painting but, philosophically, it roams far and wide. Few *genuine* books on the subject of painting ever appear. Usually they explain in easy stages how to make a landscape according to a pat formula, and the *art* of painting is entirely neglected. Carlson's idea is to imbue the student with love of nature and to open up vistas of inspiration to him—and then, to provide him with the tools of expression.

The original edition of this work in textbook form met with constant favor over a number of years and through eight editions, before this new revised volume was planned. The editors have tried to maintain the flavor of the original and all of its informational parts, adding a great number of Carlson's own paintings, placed in the book so that they bear a direct relationship to the text.

The author could hardly have foreseen the immense number of recent recruits to painting, people who paint purely for its own sake and for the pleasure painting gives them.

The "Guide to Landscape Painting" has a great deal of well-organized information that is useful to the Sunday painter or hobbyist, as well as to the professional student. The analysis of values, for instance, is particularly clear. Carlson's theory of angles is an original approach to the application of values of light and dark in landscape painting. To express a landscape in painting one must sense the large masses, feel the weight of the mountain, the hardness of stone, the floating quality of a cloud, otherwise one misses the major qualities and the picture becomes merely an organization of cardboard-like shapes. The whole chapter on angles is filled with technical but easy-to-understand devices that make clear the true values in painting. The student must be given something tangible at the start—as in this book—and then he can make his own discoveries.

Far from advocating that the tangible and the mechanical be the end, Carlson suggests only that one must have a beginning point.

This is a book to keep, to read at leisure, and to look into for the solution of problems as they arise, when the need for an experienced hand is felt. It will be a guide and aid to smoothe the way over some of the rough places in creative painting.

The experience of a painter's lifetime is in these pages, yet no book could be less pretentious. Carlson, who was a superb teacher, said the tragedy in teaching lies in the fact that it becomes necessary to make hard, concrete statements about what will merely be felt later.

—HOWARD SIMON

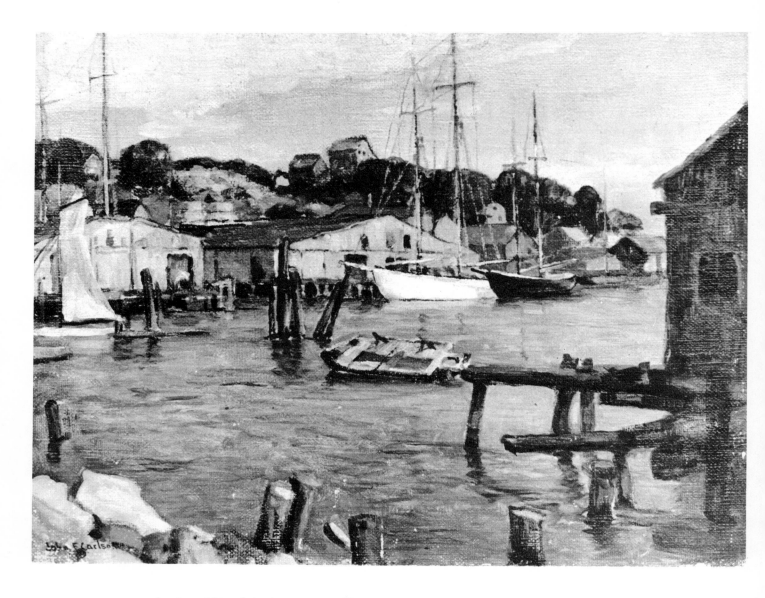

Art is a thing of the imagination. The underlying principles, the fundamentals, should be so hidden away by the beauty they are eventually to support, that it would require much digging to disclose them.

I. HOW TO APPROACH PAINTING

A lifetime of painting and of teaching has convinced me that there is a general misconception as to what art study really is. Many believe that when they are reading a scientific treatise on some department of painting, or on its history or appreciation, they are "studying art." What they *are* doing is studying the chronological sequences of the great painters' lives (which is excellent for the intended lecturer), or else studying a writer's report of his emotional responses to great paintings.

The art of painting, properly speaking, cannot be taught, and therefore cannot be learned. Only certain means can be discussed. I believe about art, as I believe about music or architecture, that the only way to *study* is to practice; and that any good teacher can point out certain intellectual or technical "makings," certain helps that will give a fulcrum to the lever of practice.

Consider how little any eulogy, or even any aesthetic treatise, will help the student who first sets up his easel out-of-doors and faces nature, with its changing, fleeting panorama of color, light, movement, sound. How shall he even begin to begin? Out of his pocket bulges a volume: "The Influence of Art Upon Society." Or another: "Does Art Uplift?" Little good will either book perform!

In this book, on the contrary, the endeavor is to present to the student of landscape painting (as well as to the lover of pictures) a few of the logical and therefore teachable aids that must underlie even the most "amateurish" approach toward achievement in this art, or toward an appreciation of the technical difficulties involved in its creation.

No one can teach "art." No one can give a singer a glorious voice, but granting the voice, and emotional sensibility, a teacher can teach a man to *sing*. In painting, as in singing, there is no excuse for a poor *technical* performance. We take it for granted that the man who is to give a concert at Carnegie Hall knows how to sing. If he does not, we do not wish to listen to him.

In painting we are apt to be very forgiving of poor technical performance. "Why, see! See what the man *intended* here!" In art, intentions have no place; only results. In good art, the results do not have to be "explained." As a matter of fact, there is but one kind of art and that is good art. There is no comfortable halfway station; it is either fine, or it is not art.

But art is a thing so much of the imagination, of the soul, that it is difficult to descend to the fundamentals of technique and yet make it plain to the student that these are but the *means,* and not an end in themselves. The underlying principles, or fundamentals, should be so hidden away *by the beauty that they are eventually to support,* that it would require much digging to disclose them. These are things we painters knew long ago, and have half forgotten. It is this that causes many teachers to attempt the impossible: that is, to start the student from the place where they, themselves, have arrived!

In this book I have proceeded upon the assumption that my readers have had little or no study, and, beginning with the bare canvas, have tried to isolate and enlarge upon the different "departments" of landscape painting until the student should have a fair idea of an approach to his task. I have tried to place these departments in useful sequence (according to their importance), taking a chapter for each. I have attempted to create a "block" or angle theory to help the student simplify, and I have tried to give the reasons for such simplification.

It is the purpose of this book to present to the student certain common sense ideas of procedure, without stifling the enthusiasm that is to carry him on. I want him to realize clearly that these ideas or rules are only beginnings; they are *means* and I want to warn him against considering them *ends*. I believe that the grave error committed in our past methods of teaching, and the thing which has caused the present uprisings against what is termed "academic training," lies in having concentrated too much on curriculum, and not enough upon the end, which is painting.

We have technically overequipped and overloaded the poor beginner. Sometimes pedantically efficient but sadly uninspired men have been allowed to stifle the young and have turned out craft-ridden automatons. Sometimes the teacher has never made it plain that he was not a god after all, but just a teacher, with human prejudices and idiosyncrasies. We have spent so much time preparing a student that when he was prepared, he was spent. What right has anyone to ask any human being to spend three or four valuable years in the "antique class" when three or four months would suffice? Three months of study from the "block" hand, or head, or figure, suffices to give the student a good knowledge of form as expressed in mass chiaroscuro, or light-and-dark, as well as a knowledge of proportion. Instantly then, into the life class, to experience the joy of the living, moving, colorful figure! Out-of-doors, into the fields and

woods, into the kaleidoscope of color and light. By and by we can return for quiet study to the antique class, and there find that we are just beginning to see and to *understand* the things we used to look at and not see.

How shall we approach our task of rendering these aesthetic experiences upon canvas so that our brother man may feel them with us? How shall we see nature with a painter's eyes, and not merely as a tourist? The word "see" does not mean, in this instance, mere visual correctness; this never in itself produces a work of art. A snapshot is a correct rendition of physical fact; sharply focused it will show the numberless grasses upon the ground; it can in fact, render these so that we can see nothing else upon the print. The actual form of the mass upon which these grasses occur, it does not suggest; nor does it convey nature's subtle color changes or color-flow. But, most of all, the camera does not *have an idea* about the objects reflected upon its lens. It does not "feel" anything, and will render one thing as well as another.

This "idea," or thrill is the unteachable part of all art. It must be intrinsic in the student. It is presupposed that anyone taking up any of the arts has this inherent sensitiveness to beauty. With this native gift, he can proceed to apply the process of reducing his material to its simplest denomination, eliminating all non-essentials, and leaving only the simplified elements with which to create and express.

By diligent practice with eye and hand (and the logical lobe of the brain), he must master the fingering of the keyboard, as it were, so that technical deficiency at least will not stand between him and expression. Once this is mastered he can very well afford to forget the fingering and proceed to play Chopin or Wagner. When one has thus arrived at the point where he can play, let him not mistake this ability or dexterity for the end or final expression.

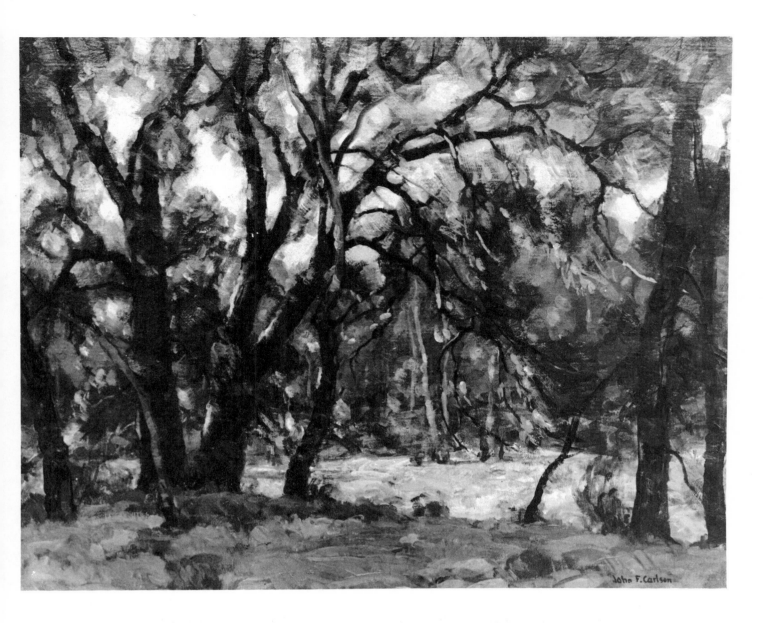

Study direct from nature. Study to *feel*, and to know something of her visible functionings. Nature, to the thoughtful, will always remain a vast and delightful storehouse, the fountain of inspiration. Nature is forever providing for the artist untabulated surprises; it is for these that he is to be envied. It is the artist's privilege and prerogative to capture these miracles and to transmute them into an expressive form.

Let me reiterate, it is only the means to an end.

Let the student realize at once that there is no method or style through which he can become a fine painter. Have not a care about "putting the paint on." Put it on any way you wish, even using the thumb, if you like, so long as you will try to do the thing I shall ask of you. You will be surprised at your own style in the course of a few months. It will be unlike anything you ever dreamed of.

Style or method in painting is like your personal handwriting; you thought little about it when you were forming your first crude letters in school. We all use the same alphabet, and one man's letters are legible to another; and yet how vastly different in general appearance! The style of your handwriting was dictated by some latent and unconscious quality within you, and even your present style will gradually change, with the years of practice in writing, or in painting, with the ripening of character. When you sit down to write an essay or a letter it is not your penmanship that you are thinking about; it is what you are going to say that occupies your mind.

The style in painting, as in writing, is subconsciously developed. You can use "thick" paint or "thin" paint; you can "stain" your canvas according to your personal feeling about it. It is what you are going to "say" on the canvas that is all-important, and not *how* you are going to put on the paint or handle the thing.

Many students become expert in "dashing" things in, while they still have little or nothing to do the "dashing" with! Let us, therefore, at the very start understand that painting is not a trick of the wrist, nor does it depend upon certain kinds of brushes. "Dashing style" in painting, unless the dasher knows intensely what he wants to say, is as offensive to those who are more developed artistically, as are the vociferations and fork-gesticulations of any empty-

headed dinner guest. Strange as it may seem to the student, the greatest things in the world are so devoid of technical ostentation, that were it not for the immensity and grandeur of *idea* in the things said (the significance and insight and the dignity of it all), they would be empty indeed.

I have often said that almost all students can *paint* well enough at the end of a season to produce a work of art. The work of art, however, is usually slower in forthcoming. The craft of painting can sometimes be acquired in a year or two, but that is but one of the means.

If you feel things intensely and can learn to see simply (which is not a child's prerogative, but that of an intelligent man), a style or manner will develop that will be adequate, and it will be as "individual" and different from anyone else's style as your personal idiosyncrasies dictate.

Your color sense, too, will improve along personal lines, and it, too, will always be distinctive and "characteristic" of you. I have never met two individuals who "saw color" identically; not only the physical construction of the eye, but the personal predilection or soul-state of each individual causes him to see differently. Copies of *personalities* are neither possible nor desirable in our world. All schools are full of the bugbear of "personality." This is often prompted by the desire in the student to become distinguished from his fellows, which is laudable enough, but which cannot be achieved hastily or artificially.

Beauty of method comes of experience and similarly cannot be forced. This leads us to consider what office beauty really fills in the work of art. What beauty in a physical sense really is, no man has yet fathomed. It is like an electric current; we use it, feel it, know in a sense how to harness it, but we do not *know what it is.*

It has always seemed to me that a picture does not rest upon beauty alone. The beauty *and* the recognized elements of subject matter (with the unity of *idea* in which they should be represented) together signify something to us; it is difficult to say what that significance is. There is a spirit behind beauty which is its cause! Beauty, therefore, must be relevant to that cause. Perhaps it is an "association of ideas," perhaps it involves what psychologists call the personal and the collective unconscious, perhaps it involves more mystical, even religious factors.

"Symbols," unless used for their aesthetic expression in line, color, or mass, have no place in art. If they do not possess intrinsic value they are mere conventions: an agreement between peoples that such-and-such is to represent so-and-so. There may be instances in the decorating of some specific building in which these symbols *must* be employed as subject matter. In such a case, if used as expressive agents of line, color, and mass, there is no reason why they should not be employed. But they become art only in the measure that they partake of abstract expressiveness intrinsic in their line, color, etc., and not because they are a convention. In this lies the difference between legitimate and illegitimate use of symbols.

It is nature that employs the first and only true symbols, the legitimate ones, when she transports us into numerous moods in which we run the gamut of emotions from laughter to tears. She accomplishes it through form, light, color, movement, sound and scent. We require no previous promptings to "understand" these things; they run through our blood, and according to our nervous receptibility, we feel them in varying degrees of intensity.

The beginner in painting begins by copying nature in all literalness, leaving nothing out and *putting nothing in;* he makes it look like the place or person or thing. By and by he will learn to omit the superfluous and to grasp the *essentials* and arrange them into a more powerful and significant whole. And it is wonderful to know that these "essentials" will be essentials to *him only* (and

herein lies the secret of originality). Another man will choose another group of essentials out of the same fountain of inspiration.

I wish to inculcate in the student an attitude toward landscape that I have called a "landscape sense." It is not enough even from our beginnings that we strain to *copy* color and form as we find them. We may succeed in doing this in a superficial way and yet not get the true sense. By the landscape sense I mean something apart from beauty, or color relation, or form relation. I mean the "*float* of a cloud"—the lightness of it, the filmy, airy thing that it is. I mean the *weight* of the ground, its *solid* massive form; the roll of the hills; the growth and reach of the trees—each a graceful, personal, individual thing.

Once you gain this idea, together with the superlative necessity of obtaining an expressive arrangement or design, you are on your way towards causing your studies to become pictures. The difference between a sketch and a picture lies not, as the beginner believes, in any difference in painting or handling. The sketch is a true statement of things as you found them; the picture is an arrangement of these things as you wish them to be. In either, the handling has nothing to do with the expressiveness.

Handling has only one virtue: by a very direct application of the pigment to the canvas, a certain freshness or sparkle of color obtains. But even this freshness of color, which gives a certain unlabored look to the picture, can only come with the *certainty* with which we paint. This certainty of value, color transitions, and forms—the "freshness," "boldness," "dash" which so enthralls the beginner—is really a detriment to his work; *not* being backed by soundness of construction or knowledge, or true artistic intention, it is offensive to those *who know,* who can see through the bravura into the emptiness beyond.

Here it might be well to touch upon the

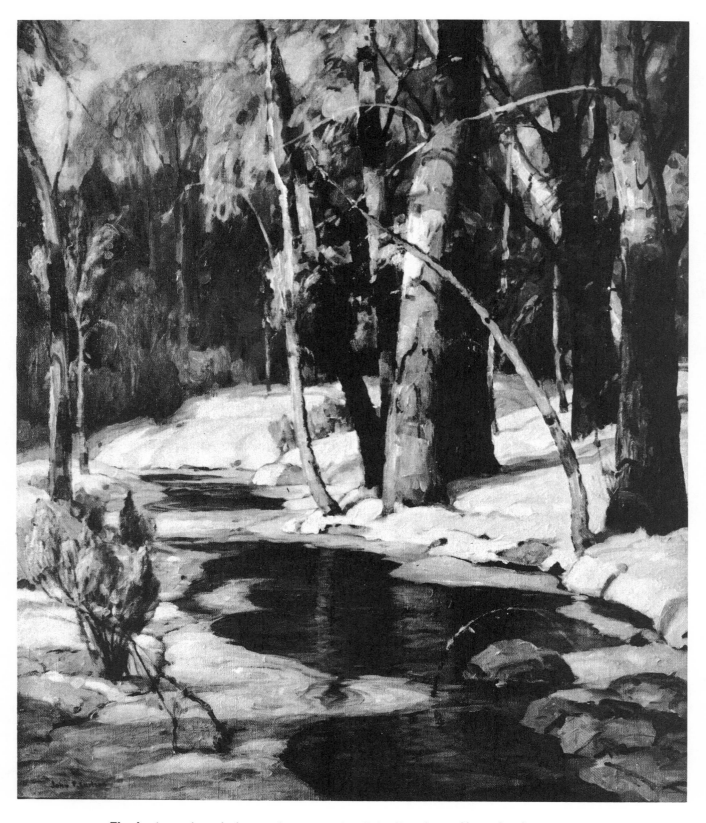

The beginner in painting copies nature in all its literalness. He makes his painting
look like the place. Soon he learns to omit the superfluous, grasp the essentials and
arrange them into a more powerful and significant whole.

question of just how large a role knowledge or intelligence plays in the production of a work of art. Mere knowledge can never create a masterpiece, but neither can "childish simplicity." The "simplicity" thesis, brought to a logical conclusion, would resolve that the youngest child would be the best artist. If so, what then is the use of living, thinking, trying, experimenting?

It is true that all great works of art are simple (as is a child's work), but the simplicity in them is not born of ignorance. Real simplicity is engendered by the insight of the artist into the abiding qualities in his motif, and an ability to choose these qualities for his use, omitting the dross. His is a superior sensitiveness, if you will.

But if mere "feeling" or sensitiveness to beauty would produce a work of art, artists would be legion. Such is not our fortune.

Power, whether physical or mental (or "artistic") comes with the *exercising* of the God-given faculties. It is difficult to go forward, but the backward slide comes with no effort. Or, to put it differently, when effort is relaxed, *we retrogress,* whether we will or no. All this does not mean that by mere hard work, or by merely growing old, one can become anything desired. There are men who work and grub incessantly, work so hard that they have not time to see! A deserving but pitiful state. The inspirational and impressional moments are shut out.

The true artist works rather in great gusts of effort, and in smaller gusts of apparent lassitude. He is not lying about "waiting for some inspiration." He is in the travail of the dreamer entering into expression.

Now when you see the artist sitting thoughtfully before his blank canvas, don't call him lazy. Realize what huge gulfs exist between a thing of dreams and the exact science of mathematics. Know that the dream is as necessary to the birth of any idea as mathematics is to the exactness of its consummation. An artist must neither be too dreamy . nor too mathematical. He must dream and he must paint.

But, first, he must know his craft. He must master the technical "makings" and he must not fear to "waste time" in studying the masters, both ancient *and* modern.

This leads me to the oft-repeated question "What do you think of modern art?" Usually the question is in a tone that suggests the wheel or rack for its followers. The answer is: A picture is a work of art, not because it is "modern," nor because it is "ancient," but because it is a sincere expression of *human feeling!* Do not think that the past is but a "junk heap," for we are the result of the past. Do not think that the future can hold nothing better than what we already have, or that change is destructive. Let us, rather, study the new as well as the old, and still be a trifle suspicious of both "reactionary" and "revolutionary" in their *extremes.*

Whatever good a new thing possesses becomes a part of our steady, slow growth. Old things cannot serve forever, nor be discarded too hastily. The past, present, and future are inseparably linked together, a moving, living chain. The inventor of the modern locomotive, for instance, cannot spurn the man who invented the wheel. Rather, he rejoices in its availability and adapts it to a new use. Initiative and "originality" went into both the simpler and the more complex inventions.

It is my hope that in this book the student may find a guide to the technical "know-how" that will serve him well in his own search for expressiveness and creativeness.

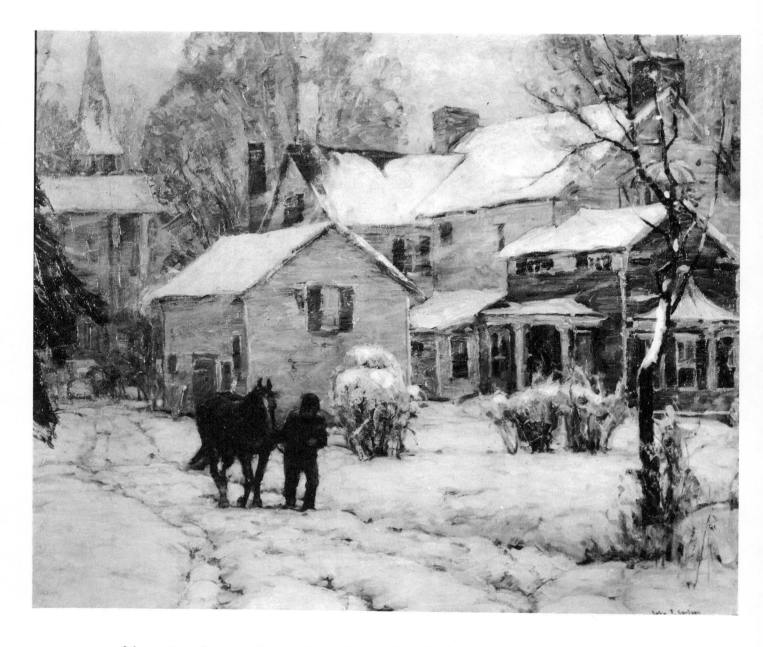

Oil painting allows much changing and correcting of color masses, until the right transitions and relations are obtained. The strengthening of the dark values (in the horse and man in the painting above) brings them closer to us in the picture plane.

2. THE MECHANICS OF PAINTING

WATER COLOR VS. OIL

Do *not* for at least the first year of your study, attempt to work in *water color,* or any other medium, but rather get your experience or knowledge in oil colors. Oil painting allows of much abuse in its handling. We can "paint in" and "scrape out" any number of times. We can lay one color over another, or keep correcting our color masses until the desired relations and transitions are obtained. We can construct and reconstruct, almost at our leisure, the portions of the canvas needing such corrections, all with very little difficulty.

With water color, the case is rather the reverse. The speed of drying of the medium requires a masterly knowledge in its uses: a knowledge of all relations, transitions, juxtapositions and constructions involved in landscape painting. The transparency of the water colors allows of no radical changes of color or composition in the picture.

The clarity of the color depends (in water color) entirely upon the directness of its application or "washing in," and since it is impossible for a student to be direct in a medium he does not thoroughly understand, I strongly urge that the beginner work in oil for a year, or until he has mastered the rudimentary difficulties of landscape painting. Once these principles of landscape are mastered, *through much experimenting* (in the more malleable medium of oil), the several other mediums of expression, such as water color, pastel or tempera will be found easier to handle.

This advice is in contradiction to the popular belief that an amateur should never essay oil painting, a fallacious theory that accounts for the many frail examples of art in our water-color exhibitions. In such examples, solidity, form and color transitions, the very rock foundation of painting, have usually been sacrificed to the maintenance of a few "clever washes," which, except for their daring, have no significance whatever. Water color is a master's medium.

For the benefit of those who have had *no* study in oil painting, I have attempted in this chapter to give what may be called purely mechanical aid. I know that in my own beginnings I would have been glad to have had suggestions of purely mechanical character.

You can order by mail, if necessary, from a number of artist supply dealers, the materials here named.

CANVASES

Needless to say, you will need for your studio equipment a canvas stretcher, a small tack-hammer, an assortment of stretcher-strips, and a roll of canvas.

Do not, at the start, attempt to paint large canvases. The large canvas requires much with which you may not yet be equipped—knowledge, traditional and empirical. Especially in out-of-door work, a small canvas is to be recommended: 12 x 16, 16 x 20, and even as small as 8 x 10. It is better for your growth to do a good *small* study than a mediocre large one. It requires so much time just to cover the canvas (if the study is large) that the intensive attention to more important factors is made impossible.

If your way of painting requires that you spend several days on one study, never attempt to paint on that study unless the light conditions are identical with those in which the study was begun. The light conditions give the "key" to your color, the unity of color relations, without which a picture does not possess "color" even when loaded with powerful pigment. I have seen students attempt to complete on a rainy, dismal day, sketches that were begun on a sparkling, sunny morning. While this is possible, if you confine yourself to the study from *memory* of form alone, or of color sequences alone, it is bad practice otherwise, because the very things that *prompted you to paint a given thing* on one day may be totally absent on the next, and your sketch becomes a pictorial hodge-podge.

Do not attempt to paint upon improperly prepared "home-made" canvas or other surfaces at the start, such as unsized wooden panels or the terrible sanded "academy board." Procure a good canvas, preferably linen, and either mount it with glue upon a cardboard (for small pictures), or stretch it in the regular way upon a stretcher. Use care when stretching your canvas that you produce an even, smooth surface; nothing is so fatal to an "inspiration" as a poorly-stretched canvas. It tests the patience of a saint to attempt anything upon it. We "cannot help it" if we paint a bad picture, but we *can* help the tragedy of a poorly-stretched canvas.

Never "key up" a canvas in a cold room nor stretch a canvas under such conditions. Both the "sizing" and the paint are brittle when cold, and future cracking is almost sure to result. As you proceed, you can paint upon anything, but I would postpone inventing any handicaps until later. A well-stretched canvas is an enticing invitation to paint. Many a picture coming up before an exhibit jury has not looked its best (nor looked like anything) because the careless

folds of the poorly-stretched canvas made the picture absurd.

Extreme care should be taken in "keying up" a picture, be it young or old. In driving in the keys or wooden edges (in stretching), be careful to establish an even tension over the canvas by gradual and equal application of the hammer upon all the keys. Never "key up" a canvas that is cold. Invisible cracks are made in its surface that will appear later. Many otherwise well-preserved paintings have been ruined by the uneven and untimely stretching of the painted surface by some well-meaning amateur, a stretching that produces a kind of torsion or "shear," rather than a tension, causing the surface (in its semi-brittle state) to crack and deteriorate.

THE PALETTE

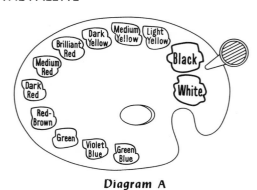

Diagram A

The "palette" or color-choice here propounded is one I have found to be absolutely satisfactory as to permanency and practicality. The colors and other materials needed are shown at the right.

For out-of-door work I find it convenient to work with the paint box on my lap. It does away with the need of carrying an easel. The strain of holding a paint box on your lap is much ameliorated if the shoulder strap is passed through the handle of the box and then strapped around your waist (like a very loose belt) while painting. This method allows you to slide the paint box fairly far out on the knees, thus giving a better view of the picture.

PALETTE MATERIALS

Paint box, 12 x 16 or 8 x 10 inches (approximate size).

One dozen panels (mounted canvas or board) to fit box.

Oil colors (choose *one* of each type):

No. 1. Light Yellow, a choice of ....Cadmium Light or Lemon.
No. 2. Medium Yellow ....Cadmium, Medium.
No. 3. Dark Yellow, a choice of ....Yellow Ochre, Transparent Gold Ochre, and Raw Sienna.
No. 4. Brilliant Red ....Cadmium Red, Light.
No. 5. Medium Red ....Indian Red.
No. 6. Dark Red, a choice of ....Rose Madder and Alizarine Crimson.
No. 7. Red-Brown ....Burnt Sienna.
No. 8. Green ....Viridian.
No. 9. Violet Blue, a choice of ....Cobalt, Ultramarine, Permanent.
No. 10. Green Blue ....Prussian Blue.
No. 11. Black, a choice of ....Ivory or Lampblack.
No. 12. White, a choice of ....Titanium, lead, or zinc white, *large tube*.

Special Notice: If Lead White is used, avoid using Vermilion and Cadmium Yellows. Cadmium Red is considered a safe color in any mixture.

Set your palette in the sequence given; ten colors in all, plus black and white: See palette, Diagram A.

Palette knife (trowel type).
Grapefruit knife, for scraping.
Small bottle Oil of Copal Varnish.
Small bottle Turpentine.
Small bottle Linseed Oil.

Folding chair or stool (preferably with a back).
Cheap umbrella (black).
Shoulder-strap for paint box.
Folding easel.

> Mix the varnish and turpentine half-and-half, and use it as a painting-medium, adding a little linseed oil when slower drying is desired. Use the same mixture for retouching, adding a little more turpentine to thin the mixture.
> Carry painting-medium in a small tin case fitted in the box.

A few yards of unbleached muslin for paint rags: tear into squares of about fifteen inches.

Painting smock, if wanted.

Bristle brushes, any good make:
   2 brushes, Number 2.
   2 brushes, Number 4.
   2 brushes, Number 6.
   2 brushes, Number 8.
Black or red sable brushes, flat (brights):
   2 brushes, Number 6.
   2 brushes, Number 10.
   1 red sable rigger (small).
(13 Brushes in all.)

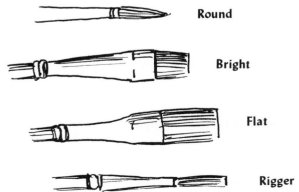

Round

Bright

Flat

Rigger

Some painters find it comfortable to carry *two* folding chairs, one to sit on, and another in lieu of an easel. Others carry a folding tripod upon whose platform the box is screwed fast, exactly like a camera. If working in very strong light, never be without your umbrella over your work. Sketches painted in the sunlight always prove a disappointment when brought into the sober light of the studio. Out-of-doors, they may seem to be sparkling with color; indoors the colors look cold and drab. Only the man who knows his palette backwards and forwards can judge his colors in the sunlight.

With the above color-palette, *any* color can be mixed. Although you can purchase fancy colors all mixed in fascinating variety, I recommend that you mix your own shades. It will keep a certain spontaneity in your color, and will sensitize your color vision. Do not stint yourself in the purchase of your colors and materials, for good tools are prerequisites in any work, and painting is difficult enough without unnecessary handicaps. Use only the colors of a reliable, standard manufacturer. A dirty palette and stiff, umbellated brushes are enough to discourage a good start, just as is a loose, poorly-stretched canvas. A master can afford to exhibit a palette gorged with old paint, but a student will find it easier to work a clean palette.

Arrange your palette in orderly sequence from warm to cold (see chapter on Color) and from light to dark—with your white placed in the most convenient place since it is most often used. I favor the arrangement shown in Diagram A, although it is only one of many ways of setting a palette.

THE "MEDIUM"

The palette given here will be seen to have a "medium cup" at its edge. The cup is sometimes called an "oil cup." Let me explain to the beginner what "medium" really is. The colors put up by the several manufacturers, in tubes, are ground in linseed oil with just enough oil to make the color flow when the tube is squeezed. Coming thus out of the tube, the color is a little too thick to be readily mixable with other colors on the palette—it is therefore necessary to have at hand a thinning-medium into which the brush is dipped when thinning is required. The palette cup holds this medium. Do not use it too freely (that is, do not mix your tones too thin) or your color will lose covering capacity and your surfaces will become viscous and slippery. The medium recommended here is an equal quantity of turpentine and oil of copal varnish.

Do not confound "oil of copal" with "picture copal." The oil of copal is the pure gum dissolved in linseed oil without any other "driers," etc. It dries hard enough to repel dust and dirt and smoke. It is an excellent retouching varnish. (Do not use the "patent" retouching varnishes, unless you know what they are made of.)

The medium described is excellent as a final varnish for a picture, but when using it as such, leave the poppy and linseed oil out of it. I always keep two or three mixtures at hand.

As men develop in their painting, they find that certain of the means hinder, and others facilitate their particular and personal method of procedure, born of experience. They even find that one manufacturer's color seems more adapted to their needs than another; that one type of brush or canvas or·medium is more to their liking than another. The likes and dislikes become so ingrained in their method that they almost pity anyone who does not see the virtue of their discovery. There is, therefore, no such thing as a "best medium." Most painters agree, however, that linseed oil *by itself* is not an attractive medium. It engenders a slimy surface, almost a greasiness that, especially in landscape painting, is not sympathetic to its textural needs. Neither is turpentine a good medium, for it causes the color to dry "flat" or dull and opaque; nor gasoline; nor kerosene.

The medium that will here be repeatedly recommended is a *mixture, half-and-half* of turpentine and oil of copal varnish, not picture copal varnish. This oil of copal medium, used as a final varnish upon the picture, dries hard, but not brittle, and will not turn yellow or "black" with time. When mixed with the paint as you mix your color, it adds body to the color, preserves or "locks" the life in it, and dries with a medium speed. When wishing to retard its drying, it is well to add a small percentage of linseed.

COLORS

The list of colors or "palette" given is one that I have found infallibly permanent (with the possible exception of raw sienna). I do not entirely recommend alizarine crimson—it is an aniline color and a too-free use of it causes it to "bleed" or saturate surrounding tones. Use rose madder or madder deep (deep rose madder).

In my own work I seldom use cobalt blue or any blue, excepting Prussian. I find Prussian blue is the only blue that retains its exact color-cast under *artificial light,* and since a picture is so often seen in such light, I deem this worthy of consideration. It will take you some time to master Prussian blue because of its "power" or saturation; it will seem to get into everything (including your everyday life), but it is an excellent blue. Reduce your Prussian blue with a little white, if you have trouble with it (enough white to make it as light as cobalt blue in value).

The question as to what kind of white to use will never be wholly settled. All whites have virtues, but I consider lead white the best—or lead white with a small admixture of zinc white.

As "collateral reading" for future use, read as many books as you can about the chemical composition of the different pigments. After you have thoroughly absorbed the knowledge of the rudiments laid down in this work, experiment with them. Work in several mediums: oil, tempera, clear wash, drawing, etching, lithography. All will tend to broaden your view and give you command of the technical secrets of these, which you may some day be very glad to possess, aside from clear artistic gains accrued.

BLEACHING

While touching upon "white" it might be in order to say that a picture (especially a light picture), if kept in a dark place for a long time (soon after it is painted), will sometimes "mellow" excessively; that is, it will appear slightly yellower when seen again in the light. In such a case, expose the picture for a day to strong light (not sunlight) in a north window, for instance, and it will be entirely purified and will never change again unless chemically impure colors were employed in its creation. The mellowing is usually the exudation of the linseed oil, or medium, to the surface of the paint. When a picture is kept in a dark place, it has no chance to bleach gradually as it is exuded. The above process is called "bleaching," and is a very valuable thing to remember.

It is well, before such bleaching, to wash the picture gently with a soft wet cloth and Ivory soap to remove any dust deposits. Use extreme care afterwards to remove every vestige of soap by repeated wipings with the cloth and *pure water.* Be careful even to wipe the tacked edges of the canvas with dry cloth to prevent the rusting of the tacks, with its consequent deterioration of adjacent canvas. Better still, use galvanized or non-rustable "tapestry tacks."

The above bleaching and cleaning process can be recommended as a restorative, in cases of old pictures hung for long periods in dark places. It will be surprising to see the color come back to pictures that have become "black" with age. After such cleaning and bleaching a very thin rub of varnish medium should be applied.

RETOUCHING

When varnishing an old canvas, the medium will sometimes run into beads (like the "sweat" on a water pipe) and refuse to go on smoothly. In such a case, take the amount of medium that you are expecting to use, put it in a separate little bottle and add to it one-fourth its own quantity of grain alcohol. Shake it into an emulsion and it will apply smoothly. When applying, do not attempt to go back with this medium over half-dry surfaces. This alcohol emulsion is an excellent thing to use as a preparatory varnish or for "oiling out" or retouching when you are expecting to repaint certain portions of an older canvas. It freshens the colors and values, creates a receptive surface and causes the new painting to be amalgamated into the paint underneath. In this preparatory varnishing, varnish the whole canvas thinly.

It will be found that a canvas that has been worked upon for several days gradually becomes very lackluster or "dry" in places. The gloss of the color seems to have sunk into the surface, leaving the surface uneven and spotty—here glossy, here mat. The actual values seem to have become disturbed. Before beginning to paint upon such a canvas, it is best to freshen the surface up by an application of varnish or oil. If the surface is too fresh to allow the *brushing on* of this "retoucher," an atomizer may be used to *spray* it on. Of course, it is not necessary to go over the whole picture—sometimes only small spots need be retouched.

For the final varnish of a picture, it is best to go over the entire surface to insure even drying. Do not attempt to go over the surface with the "medium" to insure even drying. Do not attempt to go over the surface once covered with retouching varnish until the first application is dry, or the underlying colors may "lift." If it is an "emulsion" it should be constantly mixed or shaken while being used.

Let me recommend that the medium (oil of copal varnish and turpentine) be mixed in generous quantity (pint or quart) and put on the inside sill of your studio window. This will bleach the mixture much in a week or two, although you need have no fear of its dark color ever hurting your color. The bleaching suggested is merely to forestall any mellowing of whites, if the picture should be kept a long time in the dark (a dealer's closet) or hung in an artificially lighted room. If a picture receives ordinary care, it will not mellow or crack or bloom.

VARNISHING

Much discussion has been heard about just "when" it is most advisable to varnish a picture. I believe in applying the final varnish within one month after finishing the picture (or as soon as its surface is dry enough to varnish without "lifting.") If you cannot varnish your picture within a month, I recommend leaving it unvarnished until the expiration of one year. It is the half-dry condition that is dangerous.

In varnishing a fresh picture the varnish is more or less incorporated with the pigment underneath. In varnishing a year-old canvas the pigment has become bone-dry and the varnish dries independently. Both conditions are desirable ones. Do not varnish a half-dry picture. I speak with certainty about the "medium" or varnish I have recommended. I have never had a picture crack, bloom or turn dark in the years I have used this method and material. Try to choose a clear day for the final varnishing of a picture and try to have the varnish and the picture of somewhat similar temperature. The "blooming" of a picture, referred to above, is a curious whitening of a varnished surface (a waxy-looking opaqueness) that results, I believe, from unpropitious varnishing conditions and inferior varnishes. I have not yet discovered an iota of bloom on pictures of my own of many years standing, when the "medium" here recommended was used. Do not, however, hesitate to experiment with the many different mediums, varnishes, retouchers, siccatives, oils—it may be that your method of painting requires other than the materials here given.

BRUSHES

I have often found students who attempted to paint a picture or study of modest size with brushes that were rather adapted to heroic mural decoration; in other words, too large. I have heard these students complain that they didn't seem to be able to "do anything" with them. I would advise such students to lay their large brushes aside, and to purchase five or six good bristle brushes of medium and small sizes (half of each) to use on any canvas smaller than 24 x 30. Add to these three or four *quite small* soft red or black sable brushes for the drawing of smaller touches of forms and outlines. One of these might be a "rigger" (a small brush with long hair). Naturally, as you proceed and wish to do larger canvases, you will have to add to your stock several "huskies" in the bristle line, some probably an inch wide.

There is no preference in the style of brushes to be used: the flat, the round, the long, the short. Try them all, and select those that best meet your personal needs. It is well to have varied sizes, determined, of course, by the size of the surface to be painted upon. I find it practical to use good bristle brushes for large canvases and red or black sable for small.

CLEANING OF BRUSHES

For the best care of brushes, I recommend keeping on hand a small (2-quart) pail, preferably of enamelware, filled with kerosene. Immediately after the day's painting, wash or swab the brushes out in the kerosene and wipe dry with a rag, much in the manner of a water-color brush in water. I have found this method much more conducive to long life in a brush than any other

method. For even greater convenience, I find that an ordinary small sieve to fit the inside top of the pail and extending down into the kerosene is helpful. Rubbing the brushes gently against the bottom of the sieve inundated in the kerosene facilitates the cleaning process

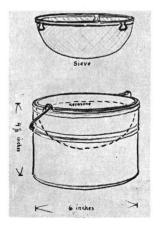

Diagram B

Never abuse your brush with soap and scrubbing. Use kerosene. If a brush becomes hard and stiff with old paint, through neglect, do not throw it away; soak it for half an hour in a good paint remover and then rinse it in kerosene. Wipe with a rag.

It is expedient to hold an old cloth or "paint-rag" in your fist, while painting, for convenient wiping of paint from brushes and canvas.

FRAMING

The frame of a picture is a part of the picture. If you have painted a good sketch, try to show it under conditions that make it possible for its whole worth to be seen. A frame should be such in character and tone as to be a transition from the wall into the picture. It should not be seen for its own sake, neither for its simplicity nor for its "gingerbread." When we have seen a well-framed picture, we never recall even the *presence* of a frame, and that is true of either a good or bad picture.

No one, however, can tell you how to frame a picture well. No law applies to it, but I dare say, if you try a picture in three

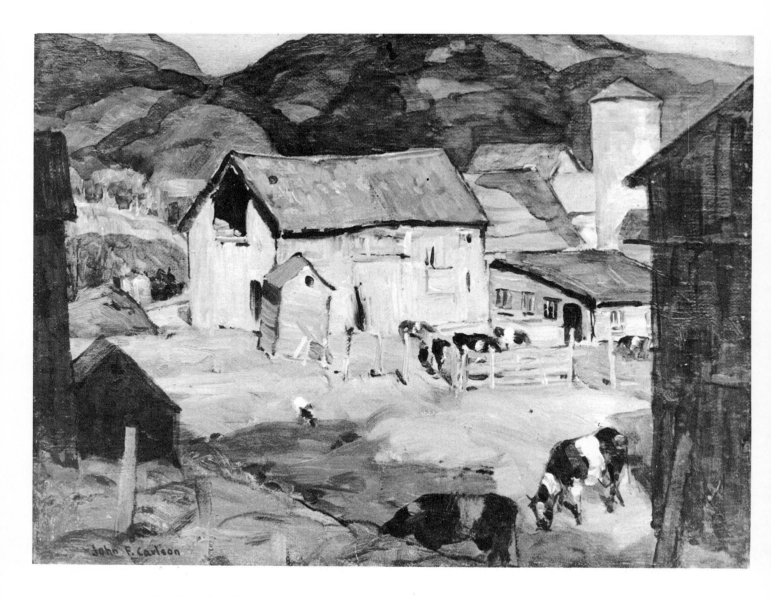

Brushes play their part in technique. A varied surface like the one illustrated here is executed with a large bristle brush loaded with color.

different frames in your studio you will recognize the best one the instant you see it. The arrogant statement that a good picture "looks well in any frame" is not as true as the statement that a good picture *well framed* becomes *more beautiful.*

While there has been a strong leaning in recent years toward white and natural frames, I do not believe that anything is more beautiful or more sensitive than a fine gold frame. I make an exception in the case of water colors or pastels, which, because of their delicacy, look best in a light frame. Gold leaf, properly toned with the desired color-cast, is a surface that seems to form the transition from wall to picture for any painting in oil; possibly because it is a slightly reflecting surface, and therefore unifies the three elements: picture, wall, and frame.

As a *practical* hint concerning the framing of pictures, I would suggest the following. Certain painters have their pet sizes of pictures and are accordingly constrained to order expensive custom-made frames. There is no real reason why a picture 17 x 22 should be better than one 16 x 20. I therefore recommend that the student accustom himself to the so-called "standard" sizes of stretchers (unless he has specific reasons to the contrary) for then the picking up of a frame for an exhibition, or for a gallery, will be an easy matter, with no loss of time.

The standard sizes in frames are 8 x 10, 12 x 16, 16 x 20, 18 x 24, 24 x 30, 30 x 40. Of course there will be innumerable times when a subject will not lend itself to such ratios and shapes as are given above; then it will behoove you to order a special frame.

SURFACE QUALITY

The word "quality," in painters' parlance, means that richness of surface and pigment that usually follows repeated applications of color upon the canvas, augmented by the use of glazes, and by "scumbling," scraping and repainting. It gives an added charm in a picture when it "just happens." It might be said that a painter who consciously tries for quality usually misses other more important virtues in his work. I think it was Millet who called trying for quality a waste of time. Yet Millet had quality. Quality corresponds to "timbre" in a singer's voice.

In painting, color-quality or color-timbre is that mysterious, personal, individual feeling for, and mixing of the *color for its own sake.* Even though ten students of mine might use identical colors to begin with, the personal vision of color or quality is so individual in each that I would guarantee to name the owner of each palette in a stack of ten palettes.

There is no special way to mix color and no special way to apply it to the canvas; neither is there any special way to "see" color. The same reaction from certain light rays upon certain objects produces varied "colors" upon varied retinas. One person cannot ever name the color of any object to the entire satisfaction of another. The nerves of the eye do become more sensitive to color through mere practice of *seeing,* much as a musician's ear is sharpened through constant practice. A painter, in seeing a beautiful mass (say of a distant mountain), subconsciously segregates the varied colors with which (to his trained eye) the mass scintillates and modulates. Beautiful harmonies and transitions are sometimes seen with the eyes closed; or as Keats says of music, "Heard melodies are sweet, but those unheard are sweeter." A picture often attains quality when the artist has thought least about it—a fatness and richness of surface, attained through repeated paintings. Quality cannot be classed as a profound, nor even important quantity in a picture; but if one grain of beauty is added to the whole through this agency, no man has a right to reject it.

TEXTURE

A picture may be painted that has color, values, composition, and quality, and yet lacks texture, or rather the feeling for textures. A flower must not "feel" like a rocky substance, or much of its beauty is lost. A painter instinctively alters his manner of painting according to the texture of the mass in hand. He caresses one surface and punches the next! A piece of velvet or linen or silk against the bony hardness of a jaw, a meadow of timothy against a rocky cliff— all *feel* different as well as *look* different. If a painter feels his textures they will become more expressive than a photographer's realism.

The arriving at textures is almost similar to the singer's "coloring" of his voice to portray certain emotions. Unless the singer feels the significance of his phrase, he cannot color his voice. So with a painter—unless he feels his textures, he will never truly "see" them.

Attempt to fit to your needs the manner of putting on your paint. Vary even the quantity of pigment according to the *kind* of texture wanted. Students love to pile on the pigment! I have seen skies loaded with great chunks of paint, and foregrounds painted with stain. The quality of both is thus impaired. *If you must* load your canvas, at least load it in the right places. This does not imply that loading a picture with pigment does any more to it than load it. Texture is much more elusive than that. There is no special way of "handling" that will help. The only help lies in your being made to appreciate its presence, and to know that it is a factor in good painting. As an experiment, try to "think" the difference in texture between velvet and silk.

While we are about it, I want to suggest that you develop the habit of painting all your "darks" with less pigment than you would use in the "lights." You may load your lights (as especially beginners like to

load). It will not hurt your picture. However, even in your light masses, do not think that mere loading of pigment is going to give you either color or form. The loading often hinders both, especially form. Paint your darks thinly, almost stain-like, to begin with; they will recede better. Most darks occur *under* forms. Keep your darks especially full of color. They need "vibration," but vibration is not mere texture of overloaded pigment.

If a picture becomes too loaded or rough in texture, in the course of its making, put it aside for a time, and when dry, scrape the too-prominent texture off, using either a grapefruit knife (curved blade), or a piece of glass with a curved edge. Varnish the picture immediately afterwards, and on the fresh varnish touch up any necessary spots. If any picture becomes so damaged that it needs re-backing, proceed to do so by removing the canvas from its stretcher, taking a fresh canvas of similar size and spreading a thick coat of lead white, mixed with linseed oil, upon its face. Then lay the picture face up upon this white surface and press evenly, all over it. A good plan is to have a piece of glass underneath, and one above, in lieu of a press. Lay weights over the whole and let it dry for several days. If any of the lead comes through to the face of the picture, it can now be scraped off with a good penknife. Let it dry for several more days, then varnish and touch up the white spots with the necessary color. Stretch upon another stretcher.

GLAZING

Glazing often produces "quality." It is a useful and beautiful adjunct in vivifying color, as well as an important aid in swaying certain tones toward a desired color unity. By a "glaze" is meant a thin application of transparent color (much like a water-color "wash") over any given surface, or more properly, over any previously painted mass.

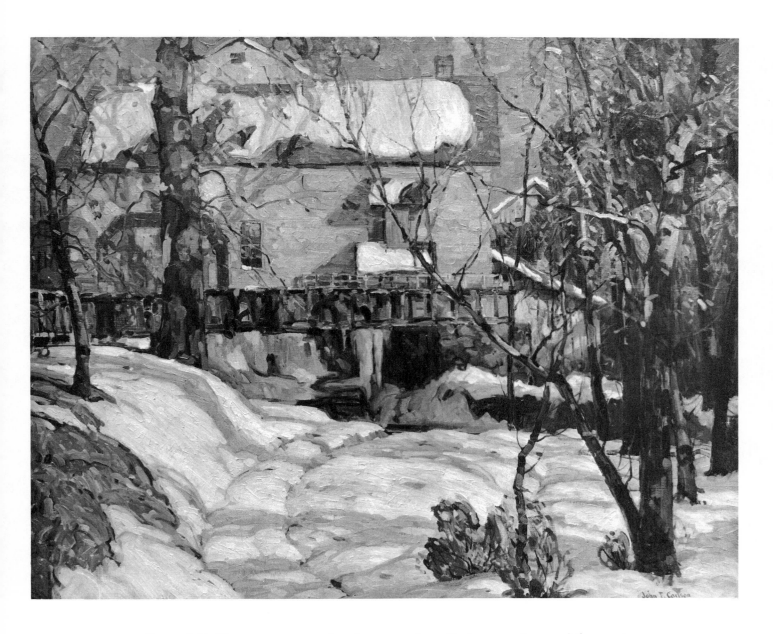

Try to "think" your textures rather than copy them. Study your edges, and the exact character at the meeting of masses, for it is there that the texture of your mass is to be found. To make a rock seem harder and snow softer, you must grasp the significant forms and textures and let the rest go. The simple statement is more forceful than much vociferation. Therein lies the superiority of a work of art over nature.

Some masters of the past relied almost entirely on glazing for attaining a great degree of color saturation. The use of the glaze can be recommended as an expedient, at least in cases where certain masses are painted and constructed perfectly, yet lack either the exact color hue desired, or the exact "value" or weight desired. Then a glaze often answers better than the entire repainting of the unsatisfactory masses.

A glaze, according to its density of color, will both darken and sway the color-cast of any given color mass. Any of the transparent colors may be used as glazes, such as emeraude green, Prussian blue, rose madder, transparent gold ochre, aurelian yellow, etc., as well as a mixture of any of these together. Suppose, for example, that in a portrait a red cloak figured very prominently; and that after the picture was about completed, it was discovered that the red cloak was both a trifle light in color, as well as lacking in richness or saturation. It is probable that a thin glaze of rose madder might easily correct this fault, and in so correcting it, would add a quality of color that *could not have been achieved* with direct painting. Or let us suppose that the foreground of a given landscape was found to be a trifle too yellowish, and a trifle light. A glaze of emeraude green might do wonders for you in correcting and beautifying it.

A glaze will not look finical or cheap, unless used as an end in itself. Men like Velasquez and Rubens did not hesitate to employ the glaze when needed. It is best when beginning to glaze to use very thin applications of it. (Like a faint water-color wash.) Even where great depth is to be gotten through its uses, it is better to give several semi-light glazes (until the result is achieved) rather than one dark glaze. The dark glaze will invariably run into the textures of the pigments upon the glazed surface and form streaky, scratchy-looking and too-apparent striations. Needless to say,

where several glazes are applied to any mass, each glaze must be dry before the next is essayed. Apply all glazes with a broad, soft brush (black or red sable) and wipe the glazed surface gently, if needed, with a very soft rag (without lint). The wiping will tend to distribute the color evenly and prevent "pools" from forming.

For either glazing or scumbling (see below) it is best to keep several small tin saucers at hand, and a very clean brush. When about to glaze, pour into one of these saucers the amount of our medium that will cover thinly the surface to be glazed. Into this medium stir a modicum of the color wanted (on the end of a small brush). It requires very little color in such a small quantity of medium to make a fairly strong glaze. In using rose madder for glazing, for instance, the mixture should look like a rather rich red wine—a little lighter or a little darker, according to your needs. Never make a glaze look heavy and obvious.

SCUMBLING

Scumbling is related to glazing and the methods of application are the same. Both should be applied when the picture is dry. A "scumble" is a glaze into which a small amount of white has been added, making it a semi-transparent or half-opaque wash. A scumble is used for reducing the value contrasts and color contrasts in a picture, when these have become too widely differentiated. The scumble will lighten the darks and darken the lights a trifle (if the lights are very light). The scumble is applied just like the glaze.

Scumbling rarely, if ever, improves the color clarity, and is apt to give the surface a rather greasy look.

Never glaze or scumble a mass unless it is well-painted. The mass should possess good construction (drawing), good texture, good gradations. When a mass possesses all those virtues, but needs a slight enrichment in color, use a glaze. If the same mass needs a slight lightening and graying of its color cast, use a scumble. If the mass is *not* well painted, *paint it over again.*

Much of the freshness and intensity of some of the old pictures was achieved through glazing pure transparent color over masses that were intentionally painted light enough to penetrate the glaze, an effect similar to that of the sky shining through a stained glass window. In our day, however, we favor the direct painting, and we recommend, therefore, that glazes and scumbles be used only as an auxiliary, rather than as prime means.

CRACKING

You will sometimes find that your pictures have a tendency to crack, that minute checks will appear after the picture is dry. This may be caused by many things: a badly stretched canvas, use of a quick-drying medium, etc. Much cracking of pictures can be forestalled and prevented if a little care is taken in the plain work of painting. I shall give but a few ameliorating "don'ts" here. Do not attempt to paint a heavy dark mass *over* a very light mass. The over-painting will invariably crack in time, and reveal by checks the white underneath. When a change in composition demands that a dark mass be painted in an area that is occupied by a light mass, scrape the light mass off the canvas with a piece of glass or a razor blade, and then paint in your dark mass. Another way is to remove the heavy light paint with a paint remover.

If you do not wish to do any of these things, glaze the light mass heavily with a dark color (after having varnished it with our medium and a small quantity of alcohol); this mixture will bite into the white mass, and the ensuing glaze will be incorporated into the underlying white. When this glaze is not quite dry, paint into it the solid color desired. The glaze establishes a kind of tough seal over the light mass and it is not apt to crack.

The best way, however, is to so *study* your composition or arrangement (or design), before beginning your picture, that vital changes in masses will not be necessary. All of the foregoing about cracking and mellowing does not, of course, vitally concern the very new beginner. His sketches or studies must, for some time, be merely experimental in character. And as to the lasting quality or performance of the things accomplished, he may even rejoice later over their very fugitiveness.

It can do no harm, however, and I would even claim that it is a *duty* in the more advanced student, to know his medium of expression. Some day he will do something that will be worth keeping, and it would be a pity, in such a case, to have mere carelessness preclude its permanence.

THE USE OF A FINDER

I have found that beginners in landscape painting have a difficult time during the first few weeks out-of-doors, in selecting and arranging their subject or motif. It is difficult to see what has, and what has *not* pictorial properties. Beginners are bewildered by the wealth of inspirational material that surrounds them, stretching away in all directions to infinite distances. They are in much the same fix as when one is trying to select a new garment, and the salesman brings forth too abundant an array of samples, thereby blunting the purchaser's faculty of choice. It is for this reason that beginners generally begin by trying to paint all out-of-doors on one canvas. Few studies are produced that stop at the few elements, well conceived, that a canvas needs. We have to learn to see.

To help a beginner learn to select, I recommend the use of a "finder" as a mechanical aid. A finder is merely a piece of cardboard (approximately 8 x 10 inches), in the center of which an oblong opening has been cut (approximately 4 x 5½ inches). By holding this mat or frame before you, a

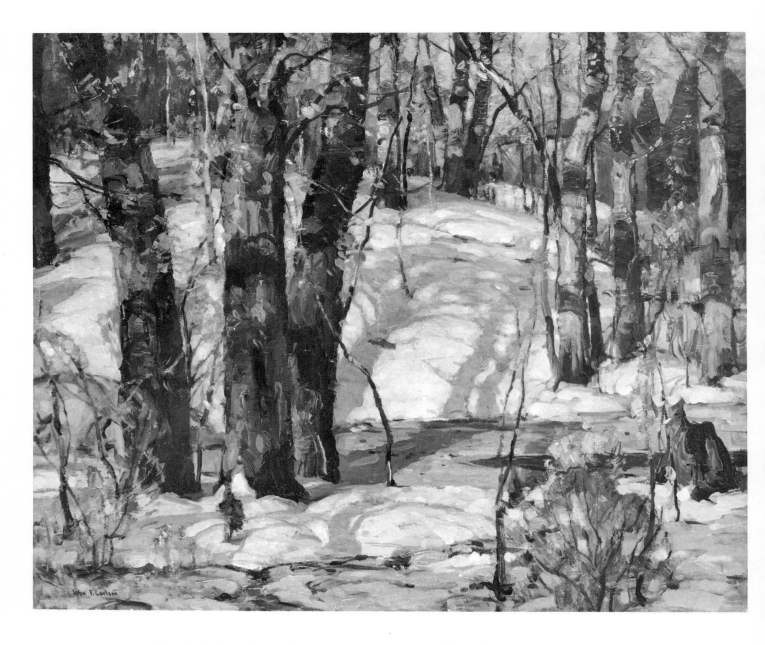

Use the finder only at the start of your painting. Before beginning look for the "big elements": sky, trees and ground. Use the finder as a frame, picking out the picture from nature's multitude of detail. Don't get lost in the little things.

foot or more away from your eyes, and closing one eye, your "motif" is shut off, or segregated from the surrounding landscape. The view in the finder will assume a picture-like aspect. If you carefully study your masses, raising or lowering the finder until an "arrangement" is arrived at, much fun, and some help will result. After you have acquired the *habit of selection,* you can lay the finder aside forever.

Selection! I have often told my students that if they would only spend as much time arranging their motif—eliminating, sacrificing, moving—as they do upon just the painting of the thing, the road to mastery would be much shortened. Most of the time I find students have planted themselves in some place that was "comfortable," or near some friendly fellow-student rather than at some place from which their selection or motif was at its best. After a time the student can, of course, paint "any old thing" from "any old place" (even indoors), but the beginnings have to be beginnings, and the student cannot start where the master leaves off.

HOMEMADE MATERIALS

You will hear much, if you travel far, about this man and that "making his own colors," or "sizing his own canvas," etc. Since art is long and time short, I firmly believe in letting the expert prepare my materials for me. The best houses employ the best chemists and workmen to produce the highest grade of materials for the artist. Why waste time experimenting with "grinding your own," when years of research would be necessary for you to produce good colors? Why spend days sizing canvas with stuff you know nothing about? Better employ the time in painting.

By all means "read up" on all these things, and know the components of your palette—what the colors are made of, and why certain mixtures of them are bad. Know all about your canvas from the time it left the flax fields until it reached your studio,

but do not make it. With your knowledge you can check up on the manufacturers and in that way, they will deliver to you only good wares. Choose a good house for your colors, and know that they are paying high-priced chemists to give you the best color in the world. Benjamin West may have made his brushes from the tail of his pet cat, but I would rather have a good factory-made brush. You go and paint and draw, and draw and paint, and then paint some more.

Don't ever buy cheap paints or brushes or canvas, unless it is imperative to the health of your exchequer. I make one exception in my tirade; that is, make your own panels.

MAKING OF PANELS

For small pictures the "panel" is the most practical—not the poor excuse for a panel found in patent fabrications of that name (that curl up when you merely look at them), but a good stout panel with good canvas *mounted* upon it.

Ask your framer to make some for you as follows: Cut some heavy beaver-board to size, and mount upon it, with good furniture glue, your favorite canvas. Then paste a heavy piece of brown paper over the back and put all under a weight or in a press for a day. This panel is indestructible and does not warp. No holes can be punched in it by careless packers. If the panel should become damaged by water, remove the canvas by soaking in water and remount on fresh board.

Do not use wooden panels to paint upon. While the texture of wood is grateful to the brush, wooden panels are very apt to split and check, and consequently ruin the painting upon them.

It may be some years before an improvement can be made upon good oil paint, ground in good linseed oil, good canvas and good brushes. Do not become accustomed to perishables; they easily become a habit.

ACCESSORIES

The student should acquire the habit of facilitating his efforts by eliminating as far as possible all *unnecessary handicaps*. There are enough *necessary* ones. When going into the field, carry a chair, an umbrella and even a bottle of drinking water. (Personally when I start out on a winter's day to paint, I am primed for all emergencies, carrying with me hot coffee, lunch, paint, spare panels, and above all, warm clothes.) For field work in winter, it is well to mix the white on your palette with a little kerosene before starting out, otherwise it is apt to be too stiff or gummy, owing to the cold.

Carry a good folding chair in the field, even when you expect to stand up to paint; a chair with a *back* to it. For small sketches (anything up to 12 x 16 inches in size), it is practical, I find, to sit down to work. In winter I find it *warmer* to sit down to paint. Do not be chagrined if you look ridiculous with earmuffs and lumbermen's boots. You will bless the latter many times during a whole day in the open, when the snow is upon the ground.

Always have a medium cup on your palette filled with our medium. Mix a little of the medium with your paint, as you work— there are times when a few drops of medium are worth a day's painting.

DOING A LARGE CANVAS

As the student progresses he should occasionally essay a large canvas. There is nothing so inspiring as a large surface of clean canvas; it gives you a sense of power. Here you *must* organize and draw and paint well. A large picture shows up *any* lack whatsoever. What was (in a small sketch) a tree, made with one touch of green paint, becomes on a large canvas a formidable mass that requires construction. Any fault of composition shoots out with cruel obviousness from a large canvas. The same composition in a sketch would be accepted as "good enough." Before beginning your large picture, spend considerable time in mixing approximately correct tones, in *generous* quantity with your palette knife upon your palette. Otherwise you will be forever mixing little stingy touches, and before you can cover your canvas, your enthusiasm will have abated somewhat, if it is not entirely gone. Get the canvas "going" all over as soon as possible, after you have thoroughly thought out your composition. A good picture is a series of good corrections, a striking of balance, so do not expect too much from the mere "lay-in."

As a practical aid in doing a large canvas, I would suggest that you do not *hold* your palette while working. Place a high stand or drawing-board to the left of your easel; upon the inclined top lay a piece of ordinary window glass about 18 x 24 inches. This improvised palette is easy to keep clean. It can be scraped without splintering. The use of the above stationary palette or painting table leaves you free to walk back from the picture occasionally. It saves the left arm from fatigue. One must feel fresh and strong to paint well!

Certain areas or spaces, beautiful while still only outlined, are often so changed when they are filled in with color, that an entire readjustment of them becomes necessary. For that reason it becomes advisable to paint masses in, *all over the canvas,* before worrying about nuances, exact hues, or impeccable values. In this mass-state the readjustment is an easy matter, for there is nothing on the canvas to spoil. Do not be afraid to spoil what you have, so long as you know *why* you are making a change. If you do not wish to venture any radical change upon your canvas, experiment with charcoal on paper. Some painters prefer to put a glass over the picture and paint their readjustment on it. When they get what they desire, they remove the glass and paint the corrections upon the canvas. This is tricky—do it any way you can.

3. ANGLES AND CONSEQUENT VALUES

Every good picture is fundamentally an arrangement of three or four large masses —a design of differing masses or large blocks of color—light, dark and half-dark or half-light. Any detail or embellishment placed within the big masses is so subordinated that it in no way disturbs these masses. Study reproductions of Giotto, and you will note this simplicity.

We have heard a great deal about "simplicity," about "elimination," about "design" in painting, but we have heard little about the how or why of it all. It is easy to say to a student, "see nature simply," but that means nothing to him. It is a difficult task to explain logically why or how he should see it simply. It is not a question of helping him to *paint* it simply, but rather one of helping him *see* it simply. If he sees it simply, he will readily find a way of painting it simply.

For his help I have laid out here a Theory of Angles. This theory sets forth my belief that the prime cause of the big light-and-dark relations in a landscape is the angle which such masses present to the source of light (the sky). Our landscapes' prime elements—trees, ground, mountains, etc.—receive from the sky differing degrees of light according to their plane, and it is chiefly this difference of plane that establishes them as darks, half-tones, and semi-lights, as related to one another. These "steps" from dark to light are called values.

Whether this theory is unimpeachable or not, it will help the student to see simply. (Diagrams Nos. 1, 2 and 3.) The student, in his efforts to create these angles, will be so occupied for a time that he will forget his preconceived idea that painting is a kind of sleight of hand or super-dexterity that is mainly occupied with putting "highlights" on grasses and leaves, etc., or with tricks of "handling" paint. As he rids himself of these notions, he will achieve the desired results. It is a curious fact that out-of-door

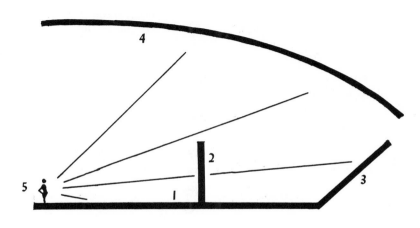

Diagram 1: **The four prime planes of the landscape. (1) is the flat-lying plane, the ground. (2) is the upright plane of the trees. (3) is the slanting plane of the mountains. (4) is the apparent arch of the sky, the source of light. (5) is the observation point.**

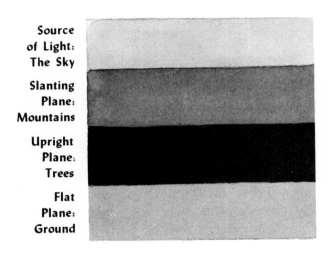

Source
of Light:
The Sky

Slanting
Plane:
Mountains

Upright
Plane:
Trees

Flat
Plane:
Ground

Diagram 2: These are the main *values* of light and dark, produced by presenting the differing planes to the light. All intermediate values are subservient to the main values.

Diagram 3: The values of light and dark in Diagram 2 are applied here to begin a picture. The values are painted in with poster-like flatness.

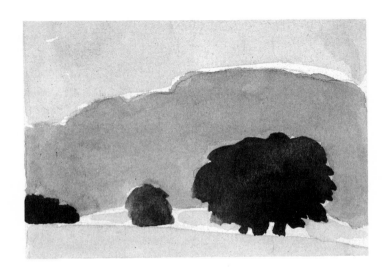

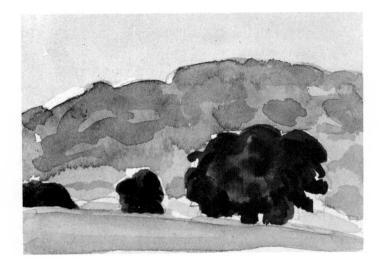

Diagram 4: The values are the same as in Diagram 3, but modeling is introduced into all flat values.

nature is to the beginner an enormously overloaded "property room." He sees for instance, the myriad leaves upon a tree long before he sees the tree at all. He attempts to paint the leaves, and the results are sad.

In landscape painting the thing that is of importance to artistic expression is the "landscape sense," a sense that makes us *feel* the weight of the mountain, *feel* the float of a cloud, *feel* the rhythmic reach of a tree, the hardness of a stone. If we do not feel these things about a landscape, we miss one of its biggest qualities. Our picture becomes a mere organization of color masses, or, perhaps, a mere delineation of shapes of cardboard. I will try in these chapters to give you something a little more than mere visualization, more than mere photographically tinting of a canvas.

Let us here, for example, analyze a tree, and see how it is related to the other elements in our Theory of Angles. The very first essential and logical quality in a tree is this: it stands more or less *upright* upon the more or less *flat-lying* ground, and *because* of its upright posture, receives a lesser quantity of light from the sky than does the flat-lying ground. (Diagrams Nos. 1, 2 and 3.) Logically, then, because it receives a lesser degree of light from the sky, it is almost invariably darker in *value* than the ground, and all this in spite of the fact that the "local color" of the tree *might* vary in color from cold bluish green to a warm olive green. I shall analyze the other planes—ground and mountain—later in this chapter.

The key to this Theory of Angles is, then, that the big elements with which the landscape painter has to deal are, first of all, light masses and dark masses, and half-light masses and half-dark masses, no matter in what sequence you name them. Secondly, that these masses or elements are light or dark, or half-dark or half-light, not because of any color-cast they may have, but because they present different angles to the light that falls upon them from the sky.

For the present we shall reduce our out-of-door nature to a colorless block-scheme of light and dark masses. Let us concern ourselves only with ascertaining whether any element or mass is darker or lighter than the mass next to it. Let us leave out entirely all detail, drawing or color within these masses. This sounds simple, but it will be more difficult than it seems. To help clarify this idea, understand at once that color-cast, hue, shade, tint, or whatever other name we may call it, is here entirely (though temporarily) separated from dark-and-light *weight* or value of the color-differences named.

We deal in this chapter entirely with the question of how dark or how light, or how medium-dark or how medium-light certain masses such as trees, or ground, or sky, or mountain, might be, as related to the other masses. We deal not at all with the question as to what shade of green certain trees might possess, nor what shade of blue or purple certain distant hills may be. We deal only in the black-and-white relations between masses; something along the lines that a good photograph of a painting possesses.

To help the beginner in determining the ratio of light and dark between these masses, he should look with almost-closed eyes at the landscape and the *masses* of differing values will be more readily seen. Once these values are established on your canvas you will find that the color and color transitions of the masses will be much more easily arrived at. In most instances when the beginner finds the color of anything "impossible," the fault lies not in the color, but in the faulty value or weight of the mass.

In Diagram No. 2 we have the simple four values in black-and-white; they represent (for our present purposes) the four big elements named above. Mass No. 1 must not be considered as a white, but rather as a light value: a pale-blue sky, for instance. All the values here given represent the average value differences of the average day in the average landscape. This value-chart suggests a very crude block of landscape. I want to make it clear here that the value-masses that we establish should represent the *middle* or average weight of any given mass and not the darkest nor the lightest spots in such a mass. The darkest spots come under the heading of "accents," and the lightest spots under the heading of "highlights."

In order to gain a thorough understanding of values it is of great benefit to the beginner to study the reproductions of fine masterpieces. Photographs in black-and-white will give better illustrations of the importance of *just* the dark-and-light design of a picture than any amount of talking; they will help more than any hair-splitting discussions as to whether the color is "greenish-blue or bluish-green." It is a curious fact that such a photograph, because of its excellent value-differences (as black-and-white pattern or masses), sometimes suggests more and better "color" than does the original painting—except a work of one of the great colorists, of course.

Proceeding with our analysis of the big planes, I shall take the sky, the source of light. The sky is invariably our lightest value, under any and all conditions, whether on a clear day when it is blue or on a partially or a completely overcast day when it is silver-gray, or warm-gray. No light *can* fall upon the different earth-planes that does not come out of the sky. They *receive* the light; the sky *gives* the light. Curiously enough this truth about the sky being lightest is most obvious on a *cloudy* day, even the most heavily clouded sky. This phenomenon is explained by the fact that, since the sky is overcast, the light that would otherwise fall upon the earth-planes is obstructed, causing these earth-planes to take on a deeper, richer, almost somber value (and color). Not only this, but since the clouds obstruct the light they are themselves lighted from above. A modicum of light sifts through the clouds or vapor-masses which retain a great

portion of the light for themselves (causing them to appear as a luminous, silvery value and color) and allowing but little light to sift through and fall upon the earth-planes. In such an instance, that is, when the earth-planes are in semi-shadow or half-light, even the *bases* of the clouds themselves are lighter in value than the earth-planes, although they appear to the uninitiated as dark and cold.

I have found from experience that this idea concerning the sky-as-a-mass and earth-as-a-mass relations is one not easily understood, even after repeated explanations. Do not be disturbed, therefore, if you find it difficult.

It is a curious fact that the value of a clear blue sky is *darker* than that of a filmy or overcast sky (except when very densely overcast as in the case of a storm sky). The explanation of this fact is easily understood. A clear blue sky has little or no vapor or moisture suspended in it. The light, therefore, shines *through* it—is in no way retained or arrested in transit—and hits full upon the solid objects on the earth's surface. A clear blue sky is like a clear piece of glass with the light shining through it, the glass itself being almost invisible. A clear blue sky is transparent, and an overcast sky is translucent; in this lies the main difference, physically speaking.

An excellent teacher, Frank Vincent DuMond, said: "The prime difference between the *kind* and *quantity* of light that falls upon the earth on a clear or cloudy day finds an analogy in the difference between the kind and *quantity* of light that is admitted through two glass doors of an office, one door being of clear glass, the other of ground glass. The clear glass admits the light unobstructed, and the light therefore falls on the floor of the room, in a brilliant patch of sunlight (showing a distinct square form of lighted floor if the glass be square). This patch is bounded by the distinct shadow-mass of the room of dark value. Note, in this instance, that the glass in

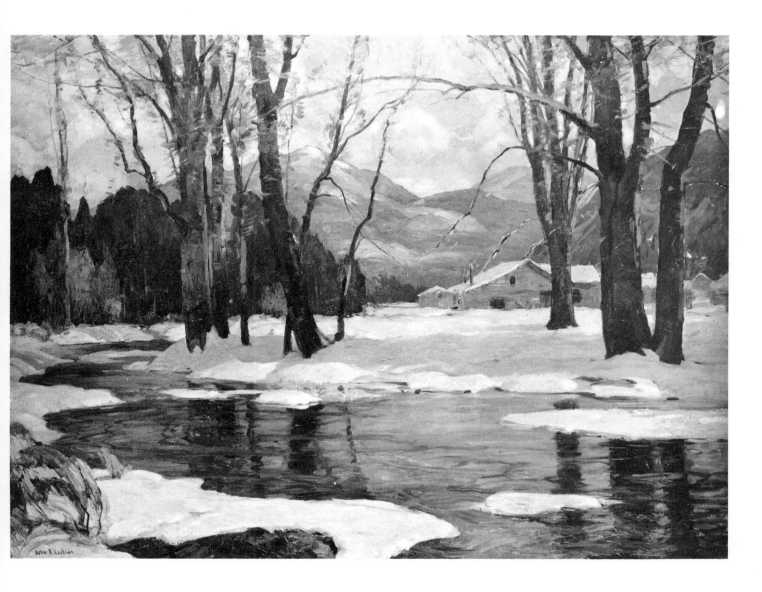

The sky, the source of light, must be the lightest mass or value in a landscape. The reflection of a white cloud in a pool of water is no exception, as all lights lose something of their brilliance in being reflected. Snow, however, is an exception.

the door (being clear glass) *retains* none of the light for itself, but is lighted through and can be looked through like clear water. Compared with the piece of ground glass in the other door this clear glass does not radiate light, but allows the light to fall sharply upon the floor.

"Note, in the second instance, that the ground-glass door admits a not so direct light, nor so brilliant a one, but it seems to diffuse this light all through the room in a more luminous way. The ground glass itself in the door is of such a brilliant light-value that one can hardly look at it with open eyes. The light is *held in the glass* by the thousand minute facets of the 'ground' and is diffused into the room. There are no *marked shadows* (only vague ones) nor any brilliant light-patches. The glass of the door is the most brilliant *light* in the room."

"Ah!" someone will ask, "but what of the days when the storm-rack or nimbus clouds almost obliterate the landscape? Then, *surely,* the clouds are darker than the earth."

This argument is equivalent to saying: "The less light that falls upon a mass (the earth), the lighter it is." It comes from having seen an instance of a stormy day when a break in the cloud-racks actually admitted sunbeams through this break. In such an instance the brilliant *spot of light* that fell upon the earth was, of course, the most brilliant thing in the scene and much lighter than the low-hanging clouds. Let me add, however, that were the same sunbeam to fall direct upon one of the clouds, the light *on that cloud* would be lighter than the light on the ground. For, after all, the same light falling upon a cloud would produce a warm white, but when falling upon any of the ground elements would produce a rich yellow-green, orange or red (of medium value), or any color you can name—all of which would be darker in value than the above warm white.

The foregoing has been concerned mostly with the sky. The earth-elements are our next interest—the *semi-light* value of the ground or flat-lying plane. You will note in Diagram No. 1 that this plane lies exposed more directly to the light of the sky than any other earth-element. In consequence, it is usually the lightest mass in the landscape, barring the sky. Remember that consideration has been given to the fact that all these planes may possess a variety of modulation, undulation, or variform, each plane within itself, and that these variations within each mass may appear to confound one plane with another. They seldom, if ever, do so. The seeming half-steps of value within each large plane will be found, upon closer analysis, to belong to one or another of the main large masses. For artistic reasons they should be *made* to "belong."

Again, the light from the sky falls *most* directly upon the ground or flat-lying plane and consequently raises or lightens that element in value. This is true, regardless of the differing local colors of objects, such as bare earth, grass, stones, grain fields, flowers. It is, therefore, important that in spite of the great color difference of the ground objects just named, they be so held in restraint as not to destroy the generally light-flooded flat-lying plane with any too great differences of light and dark.

With this idea mastered, it is remarkable what tremendous color-difference on the ground can be handled in *confirmation* rather than in denial of its special plane. And do not confuse the undulations, rollings or forms of the ground with the upright planes, for the undulations belong to the ground-value and are only slightly darker than the general mass upon which they occur.

Try to see that elements of which a foreground is made are not a conglomerate mixture of material such as grasses, flowers, stones, bare earth, etc., but rather a decorative arrangement of these. These elements are usually grouped or "colonized," as I call it. Like begets like in these elements. Goldenrod, daisy, devil's paintbrush, Queen Anne's lace, different grasses—all seed themselves close to each other and therefore result in beautiful patches of this, that, and the other. They lend themselves, therefore, to the painter's needs. These groups conform to the configuration of the ground and to the law of perspective. (Diagram No. 23, page 79). This is a most important fact. It will forever do away with the mere "spotting" of a foreground with a pot-pourri of meaningless paint spots. We get, without knowing it, the ground (as form), detail, decoration, and the third dimension.

Even if you see foregrounds that do not have any easily noticeable groups, you must take whatever elements there are and group them. Nature can afford to mix things up, but a picture must be an ordering of the material into masses. We must have design in a picture even at the expense of truth. You are *using* nature for your artistic needs.

Care must be exercised in painting these areas of different colors (and slightly differing values) so that the values do not differ enough to infringe on or conflict with the upright plane or trees. The upright planes should be darker than any of these modelings upon the ground. The trees must appear as masses against the ground. Not only are trees darker, as a rule, than the ground, on account of the plane presented to the overhead light, but also on account of the actual *local color* of most boscage or foliage (or even bare trees) which is of cooler color than any of the other ground elements.

Much care should also be exercised in refraining from putting lights or highlights upon trees (lest you endanger or even destroy their uprightness of plane. The spotty appearance of the beginner's trees is almost always due to this abuse of these vertical masses with spotty highlights. This would almost seem to discourage the modeling or forming of the upright planes. But the student will find that by having the upright planes definitely and generously darker

than all other planes, a comparatively slight variation of light and dark will suffice to model their form. Especially is this true when this variation in value is coupled with a close study of the color changes within the value-mass.

Beware of the darks within the dark masses, such as the inside shadows of the tree. The general tendency is to make them too black.

Both accents and highlights on any mass, used sparingly, will "tell" without encroaching upon any other value-mass or plane.

After we thoroughly understand the big planes, thus keeping our picture simple, we will readily discover just how much we may encourage the half-planes without chopping up the big planes or masses. The "suppressing" of these half-planes (which causes half-values) finds its counterpart in the painting of a head or figure. We so suppress the "half-tones" as to cause them to belong to the light on the head rather than allowing them to remain "half-darks" that verge on shadows, which would make the head an "over-modeled" thing.

There remains for us now in our Theory of Angles, to examine the third earth-element, the slanting plane; that is, hills or mountains. The mountain, because it presents in the main (or in spite of its many variations of slope) a slanting plane to the light, is approximately a semi-dark value, somewhere *between* the value of the ground and that of the trees. (Diagrams Nos. 2 and 3.)

We know that, geologically speaking, a mountain is composed of a great variety of slants and planes—of precipice, tableland, cavern and spur. All these planes have this in common: they rise at varying speeds from the flat, gradually reaching an apex, and then as varyingly descend to the flat. These variations we put under one head and call the "slanting plane."

I am referring here to the lower verdure-clad mountains of the East, such as the

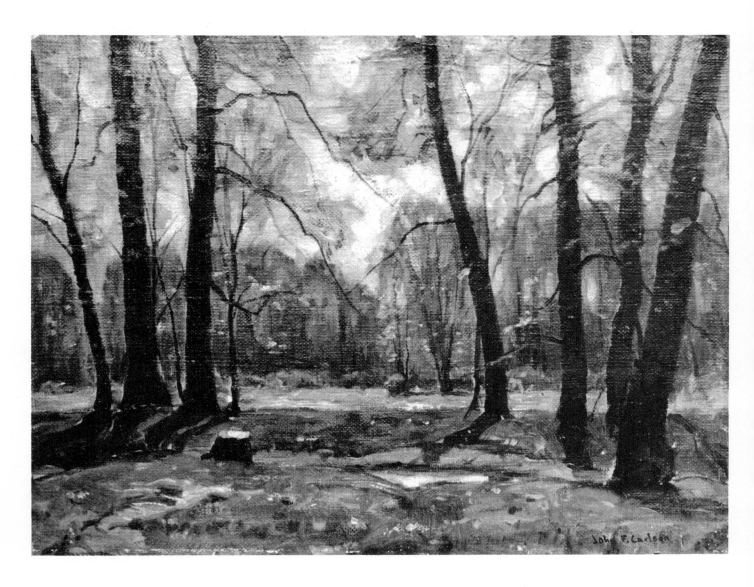

The trees which form the upright plane should be darker than any modeling upon the ground. The trees must appear as masses against the ground. The rest of the landscape here is subordinated to the great forms of the trees.

White, Adirondack, and Catskill Mountains, which are not too big to be seen at near range. The semi-dark value for mountains would not hold in the case of some sandstone and granite mountains of the West. Their "local color" is much lighter in value than our forested mountains of the East. These western giants can only be seen at much greater distances than the eastern hills, on account of their stupendous size. These giants, at this great distance, are so lightened or hazed by intervening atmosphere that they become a pale blue or violet, nearly, but not quite as light as the sky, and when snow-caps exist, much lighter than the sky. But even under such conditions the nearer foothills retain their identity as slanting planes and half-darks.

Let us briefly sum up: We have arranged upon the canvas (from direct study of nature) four or five large flat tones of unequal weight, in the light-and-dark sense (values), and have tried in so doing to follow nature as to the different colors of these masses. For instance, we have the blue of the sky, the darker violet or blue-green of the mountain, the still darker green of the trees, and the semi-light yellower-green and grays and warm pinks of the ground. We have arranged them in a poster-like flat design, a very desirable beginning, indeed. For we can soon proceed to the beautification of these value-masses through the addition of color—correct local color, subtle variations and gradations of this local color; the vibration of color within the masses, etc.

All these elements, with their related value-differences, placed upon the canvas as *flat tones,* are the beginning or the makings of the design. We shall discuss their distribution and areas later. When properly related as weights they function doubly in that they create a design and at the same time become the "block" layout of the essential elements of the landscape. If made beautiful in form or shape, they function decoratively. The landscape is thus simple, because only the essential masses have been tried for. If we can keep this simplicity throughout and still add the embellishments of color, form, gradations and, finally, enough detail, we will be in a fair way to enter into artistic considerations.

There probably never was a picture that was poor because it lacked detail or subject-matter; rather the opposite. Bad paintings are usually so overloaded with useless detail that the essentials are obliterated.

To prove to yourself that the angles described above have more to do with the value of any given mass than the local color of that mass, bend a fairly stout strip of white paper into three differing angles (see Diagram No. 1) and note the distinctly marked differences between those planes, in value. (Hold the paper in a manner that would represent the flat, upright and slanting planes of the landscape under the sky.)

Our landscape, thus far, is a design in two dimensions, that is, it has height and breadth, but not depth, form, or volume. It is lacking, too, in color. These lacks are to be made up soon. As a *beginning* the principal "form" is the angle that the big elements create, one with the other, regardless of what other forms are incumbent upon these planes or angles. Were we to "build form" in a landscape before appreciating the big angle on which the form or forms appeared, it might be like putting our rugs on the walls and our pictures on the floor.

Since there are exceptions it might be well to repeat here that the suggestions laid down are those governing the *ordinary* landscape in an *ordinary* everyday light. There will be innumerable incidents when the Theory of Angles will be disturbed—even annihilated—but the student, after understanding the general rule, will be better able to cope with the specific exception. The habit of analyzing the weight or value of any color-mass will stand him in good stead when the unusual happens. The habit of thinking in terms of value or angle to begin with, even though one should run riot in color *afterwards,* will be proven of benefit, whether we paint landscape, portrait, or still life. Even when the unusual does happen—as, for instance, when the setting sun shines *along* rather than *upon* the flat-lying plane—thereby causing the upright planes to receive more light than the flat-lying planes—it is still the angle that determines the value-revision, thereby proving the theory.

It is the *natural* elements to which the theory applies, and not any *man-created* elements of the out-of-doors, such as houses, fences, etc. Obviously enough, a house could be white and therefore lighter than any sky-value or flat-lying plane among the natural elements, even though it is an upright plane!

The only "rule infallible" is that a picture, to have a design, must have value-differences or simple light-and-dark masses within it.

The places assigned to the values named are sometimes (though rarely) turned topsy-turvy, and with good effect. There are times in early spring and in late fall when the trees are a pale yellowish-green or faded yellow (local color), respectively, and in both instances lighter than the ground; but being lighter than the ground they still persevere a very light *but darkly accented* mass, as an upright plane. Sometimes, too, a cloud shadow might, when falling upon the ground, leave the trees in light and the ground in darkness (and thereby reverse our values), but this accident need not be feared. The remaining planes in the picture being *just,* they will explain the incidental and temporary reversal.

The rule is also annulled when there is snow upon the ground, for then the white mass of the snow is much lighter than any *part* of the sky excepting the sky *near the sun.*

If the student will once recognize the general and everyday value-differences in anything, he can easily see for himself any incidental departure from this common condi-

tion. He will in time despise any "rule" concerning painting.

I have no desire to lay down rules of procedure for starting a canvas out-of-doors, but I feel I must provide the beginner with some mention or hint of *one* way.

I discourage any elaborate drawing-in of the motif to be painted, either with pencil, pen or brush. This produces a fear of the pigment or paint; a kind of dry, joyless "working up to the edges," and leads subsequently to a kind of "colored drawing."

I think it best to proceed (once you have something that interests you) to draw roughly upon the canvas, with a half-sized brush, a bold and thick outline of your main masses in any semi-dark color (just to get your big design). Instantly fill in these masses with their approximate color-contrasts, taking care to weigh each mass as to its exact value. Use a full brush, for it is easier to "play" the color-differences into a given mass when there is enough pigment on the canvas to receive it. If you are using the varnish-medium, elsewhere prescribed, you will find that the paint dries fast enough in an hour or two to permit of "dragging" other colors over any given mass.

Do not leave any bare canvas showing between the masses of color, for this method in the hands of a beginner engenders a "fussy," spotty, dry feeling in the color. Bare canvas simply confuses you unless you know your values pretty thoroughly. Keep a palette-cup on the edge of your palette and thin your paint a little with the medium in it as you work along. For the first scrub-in of your picture you can use the good bristle brushes, but for repainting, especially in fresh paint, I recommend the square black sable brushes; these will not "lift" the underpainting.

One mysterious thing to beginners is the shadow cast by one plane upon another; for instance, the shadow of a tree upon a meadow, or a cloud upon a mountain. "What color are they—what value?"

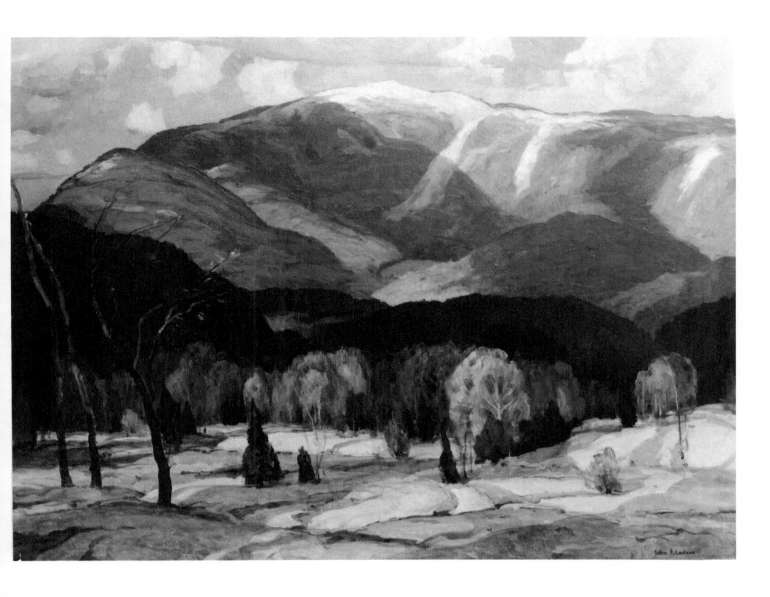

Try to feel that almost all natural, growing forms are convex lines rather than concave. Many a mountain outline has been spoiled by being made concave. All earth-forms bulge up, as it were. The mountain rises, the ground swells, trees tower. Concavity creates a "hanging" line, and unless it is imperatively needed for artistic reasons, beware of its use. Note the heroic forms of Delacroix and Michelangelo, and you will see little concavity present.

All beginners paint these shadows *too dark*. Allowing that the shadow cast by the usual green tree falls upon the usual field or meadow, this shadow is usually much lighter than the tree which casts it; *much lighter in value*. This is mainly so because the shadow falling upon the flat plane is exposed to much reflected light from the sky, a cold light that sifts into it. The exact color of the shadow is, of course, determined by the *local color* of the field or flat plane upon which it is cast. Whatever this local color is, the shadow falling upon it assumes the same colors, except that they are of a darker value. Remember, too, that the sky reflects a cold light (the sky being necessarily blue when such shadows exist) into the local colors of the shadow, thereby cooling its whole color-cast. For the same reasons there is a slight warming of the color of any shadow as well as a slight darkening of its value as it approaches the tree casting it, due to the fact that, as it approaches the tree, the shadow is less and less exposed to the cooling and lightening influence of the sky-reflection.

Another consideration of our shadows is that of their color and value changes as they recede into the distance. I find that many students have the mistaken notion that "all shadows are blue." For this reason I wish to make plain the logic of receding shadows. You will find in the chapter on Color the statement that all colors, as they recede from the eye, grow cooler (or bluer). Naturally enough, our shadow conforms to this law of color. A shadow seen falling on a distant mountain, for instance, is infinitely "bluer" than a shadow from a tree upon a foreground meadow. The shadow on the distant mountain is bluer, *not* because it has more sky-reflection in it, but because *it is a distant object*: it is seen through an intervening veil of atmosphere that cools it along with the other objects in that same distance. This fact, and the fact that it gets its proper share of sky-reflection, makes it quite a blue

thing indeed. Thus, if the distant shadows are quite blue, and the foreground or near shadows retain their local color (only slightly blued), it is easy to understand that any shadow falling on intermediate spaces or middle-distances is, of a necessity, of a color and value lying somewhere *between* the *extremes*.

I want to mention here, too, that while these shadows get "cooler" as they recede from the eye, they also (along with all the other values) get *lighter*. This will be hard to see at first, because for some reason that I have not been able to discover, all cold or blue colors appear "very dark" to the beginner and all warm yellows, orange-reds and brilliant greens appear "very light." This curious and common idiosyncrasy is responsible for more failures to realize values than any other cause.

You will find that if you can master a shadow in the manner prescribed it will look luminous and not black. A thing that adds much luminosity to any shadow, too, is the proper use of dark "accents" within it. These accents are the only real *darks* in a shadow. They represent such things as the very dark *dark* that might show under the edge of a stone (lying in the shadow) or the dark under the roots of tufts of grass or a small bush within the shadow. These accents are very *faint* in distant shadows—in the great distance hardly existing at all. Needless to say, the accents referred to exist even more pronouncedly in the full-lighted areas in meadow and tree, or even in the mountain and sky. They represent the small hidden-away places that receive no light at all, or nearly no light. They are prone to be very dark in foreground elements.

And while we are touching upon "other values" we might as well consider an important fifth value, and add it to our other four. I refer to clouds in a blue sky. Aside from their expressive qualities, such as movement, lightness, etc., they form a beautiful pattern of bright light upon an already bright blue value-mass. Their character, color, etc., will be treated in the chapter on Clouds. One word concerning this fifth value: when there are clouds present in the sky, their brilliant white almost always causes the beginner to paint his blue sky *too dark;* then, in order to get any kind of just relation between his sky and the land, he is forced to jam all his land values into the appearance of a cloudy, dark day. There is not so much difference in value between the blue and the cloud in any sky as we are led to believe. Most of the blue skies brought in by beginners are dark enough for a moonlight night. I have never seen a painted sky that gave the impression of being *too* well lighted.

In this chapter I have continued to speak of "four big elements" as though *every* picture must be made up of these. You understand, of course, that such is not the case. We might be painting a desert, for instance, where only sky and earth prevailed, with possibly some other darks, such as rock masses. There would be but two large value-masses in such a picture. These two masses would, however, conform to a law of relation just as much as though the other planes were present. Because of this they would require much more discernment than if the other planes were present to lean on, so to speak. What we desire is *masses,* whether there are two or ten.

Remember this, too, that every day has its own gamut of values. Some days are dark and mysterious, others light and moving. Try to see how the gamut varies, but do not think that the values are destroyed by this variety. Obviously enough, the differences between dark and light masses on different days are seldom the same in *degree* of separation. On a foggy, "silvery" day, for instance, the difference between the darkest mass and the lightest mass is not very great, owing to the fog lightening all the darks, or raising them in value. The middle values (ground and mountain) are therefore difficult to fit in between the lightest and the darkest masses. Remember that no matter how delicate a picture may be in its contrast of values (meaning the scope between the *lightest light* and the *darkest dark*), these values retain their identity absolutely within the given key or scheme; in other words, they never become jumbled. (See Diagrams Nos. 6, 7 and 8.) Even a star-lighted landscape possesses clean-cut mass-relations.

The arrangement or composition or organization of these masses of value—these "makings" for our future expression will be treated in the next chapter on Design and in the chapter on Line. I recommend that the student experiment in black-and-white with the principles expounded in this chapter, first using charcoal, crayon, or sepia.

It is an amusing fact that students will run for miles to paint something which they think *denies* the thing the teacher is trying to tell them: some simple accident that no one can deny. Were there under God's sky a spot where trees grew with roots in air and branches in the soil, there would we find bevies of students painting!

I repeat: do not model, embellish or load the big constructive value-masses with detail which spots them or confounds them with other masses and you will arrive at true simplification. In other words, do not make differences *within* the big values that are so contrasted that they break up the mass, but hold such differences in check.

In studying any good picture we find that it might easily be dissected into four or five large value-masses with the necessary detail or embellishments superimposed upon them.

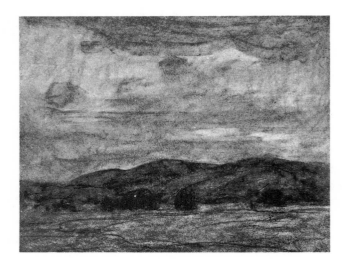

Diagram 6: The ordinary overcast day. In it we find the sky a turbulent light-grey mass, with the cloud bases more darkly marked. The earth is in shadow, consequently rich and dark.

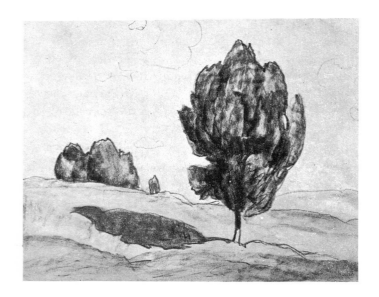

Diagram 7: The ordinary sunlight effect. The sky is blue. Because the ground is brilliantly lighted, the difference of value between earth and sky is not so far separated. The shadows are the only real darks in it. They are crisp and well defined.

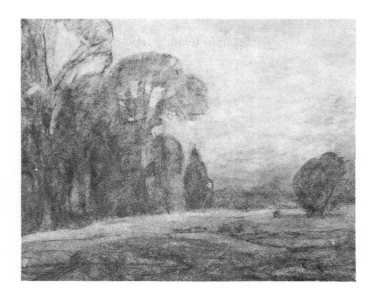

Diagram 8: The foggy or silvered day. The values are brought close together (but not confounded). The whole scheme is light and airy.

4. DESIGN

A Pattern of Differing Values

Now that we understand the material with which to make design, let us proceed to distribute this material upon our canvas in a "decorative" way—that is, let us make a design out of our basic masses of planes.

Let the student take one of his sketches and, with the material before him, arrange it on another piece of canvas in such a way as to be more expressive of the idea he had in mind when he began his sketch. Do this in the studio. In thus analyzing his idea, he will discover that the sketch contains a lot of useless material, and that what is left could be much beautified and the idea strengthened by a totally different distribution of his main masses. If he succeeds in this, his canvas will have come nearer to being a picture. (I shall explain this at length later in the chapter.)

Before going further, it will be well to inquire into the meaning of the word "decorative." *Variety* of shapes and sizes may be said to underlie all good decoration or ornamentation. In the chapter on expressive composition, we deal with the *kinds* of shapes, a matter of feeling. Here we deal with shapes from a more cold-blooded viewpoint, that of their areas and their distribution. While this decorating of surfaces is admittedly a somewhat superficial thing, a fine picture can seldom be said *not* to possess it.

Decoration is not the sole aim of art, I admit. Just because a thing is beautifully wrought or arranged does not mean it has reached its limits of expression.

By "decorative composition" is meant the arrangement of value-masses into a design, almost as a poster designer would proceed. It means weighing your masses as areas and arranging and balancing them into a pattern that will be interesting and beautiful because of the infinite variety of shapes, lines, and sizes, and the forms of these. In the previous chapter we discovered how to create the big angles or planes. We consider now how to arrange these things or elements into an orderly result. It has been said that nothing depresses the soul so much as perfect symmetry. Symmetry is static; variety is dynamic.

Proportion is the soul of architecture and art, and if we can *view* our "decorative composition" as a study in proportion we will have gained somewhat. A thing becomes "interesting" when it is well proportioned, possibly because all finely proportioned things function better than misproportioned ones, and we are interested in things that function well.

Each individual *must* be guided by his own feeling or taste in this matter; formulas might lead to deadly repetition. But mixed up with our "feelings" about anything, there is a certain proportion of reason. Reason never produced a work of art, but in all true works of art there is a certain amount of very sane reasoning (subconscious though it be).

I know that an artist could tell, were he questioned the instant he drew one line on a canvas, exactly *why* he put that line in a certain spot. There is, then, a reason for the placing of every line. There is no irresponsible or accidental child's play about the composing of a fine picture. Men like Leonardo, Michelangelo or Rubens were men of fine intellect as well as of sensitivity. Pure beauty is an orderly quality which seldom emanates from imbeciles or charlatans.

Let the student when beginning a study (after he has been *inspired* to paint by some vision of beauty in nature) calmly decide while he is setting his palette just what it was that inspired him to paint that thing, and how he can make it evident upon canvas. In other words, establish the *idea* in his conscious mind and then compose *for* it. Reason out how to arrange the masses upon the canvas so as to *help* that idea rather than hinder it. I have often had students say to me: "I really wanted to paint that mountain, but *before I knew it* those trees took up the whole canvas!" My advice would be in such an instance to begin a new sketch, and consciously give the mountain its place and its preponderance in size and dignity, using the trees as a mere accessory (or making them smaller in mass).

When beginning to sketch, be careful how you place the first few touches or outlines of your masses. You may either make or break your picture in those first placings. There is nothing so discouraging as a bad composition at the very start. Do most of your "changing" in composition before you begin to paint, for at the beginning, when you are fresh, it is easy to change a composition. It is just "blocked in," and there is nothing to "spoil." (See Diagram No. 3.)

After you have begun to paint, it is very difficult to have to make radical alterations in arrangement. An artist-photographer once remarked to me: "We have to do all our work before we snap the shutter." (He meant, obviously, the arrangement, contrasts, etc.) Before the student begins to paint, let him "draw in" simply the big contour or outline of the masses (with brush and paint and some semi-dark color), enlarging this mass, reducing that; changing the direction or slope of this mass, and that; "weighing" the masses back and forth until the desired arrangement is arrived at, or until the variety of relative sizes and shapes and lines not only gives to the central idea its proper importance of size, but also produces a decorative and interesting "design" through its variety of areas.

Don't paint "direct from nature" when all elements of organization and beauty or design are palpably absent.

Find another motif—a motif that will lend itself to pictorial ends. Nature is seldom perfect in design. The artist must look to nature for his inspiration, but must rearrange the elemental truths into an orderly sequence or progression of interests. By "sequence" is meant giving primary, secondary, or tertiary importance to such forms and color masses as are needed for an end and leaving all others out. In speaking of composition the use of the word "need" may sound enigmatic to the beginner. Let it be understood, then, that since nature is rarely perfect in design quality, the artist, in rearranging his "natural" elements upon the canvas, is creating a picture. This may involve moving objects to left or right, raising or lowering the horizon, slanting a mountain's contour in a direction opposite to that of nature, enlarging or reducing various masses, strengthening or reducing certain lines, introducing minor elements such as stones, bushes, fences, flower-patches, etc., to give a desired *line;* "placing" clouds in a manner to emphasize their sweep and movement to coordinate with the other lines of his picture. He is really using nature and her forms, while he manipulates the natural truths to suit his artistic needs. Were this not so, the man who could slavishly imitate or *copy* nature as he saw her would be the greatest artist; but he never is.

Study nature carefully—note what is taking place upon the face of nature; watch for the subtle transitions of color and paint these things, arranging them to best express a subjective idea. Otherwise you might as well use a camera.

No law or formula can be concocted by which good composition would always be assured. I can only suggest that the student experiment with charcoal and paper (with any given motif in mind) until he feels that *one* arrangement out of the several made embodies his idea better than all the others combined, and that he then try to decide *why* it is better.

Differing proportions or variety of shapes and sizes is the requisite of decoration. In the very first "drawing in" of the big shapes in a motif, be careful how you divide and subdivide your spaces. The *largest* spaces will always demand more attention from the eye than lesser ones (even when the latter have brighter color or greater value contrasts, intrinsically). Compose, then, for the thing that you deem most important by giving it the preponderance of space. The next mass in sequence of importance need not be the next largest—it may instead be most important in color and value, and so on down the line. Do not divide your canvas into equal-sized spaces unless you do so for a definite artistic reason.

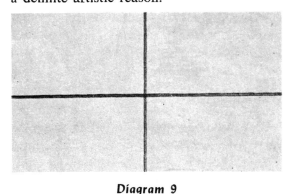

Diagram 9

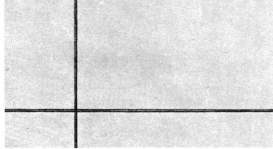

Diagram 10

In the rectilinear divisions of spaces shown here, I am indebted to Arthur W. Dow, who promulgated the "Scotch plaid" idea of space-division (see Diagrams Nos. 9 and 10). Obviously enough, a canvas that is divided into equal spaces (Diagram No. 9) is less interesting than one that is divided unequally (Diagram No. 10). In No. 9 the shapes (and their sizes) are similar. In No. 10 there is variety of shapes and sizes, even though they are limited to squares and oblongs. Diagram No. 11 is the same as No. 10, except that four more lines have been added. These four lines have been so placed that they add further variety of spaces to the whole, besides introducing the inclining line. By adding the inclining line we have added the triangle to the squares. If a curved line were added we would be adding still more to the variety of shapes and sizes; and so on, ad infinitum. Compare all this with Diagram No. 9.

When you see something that interests you to paint, do not flop down in some cool, convenient spot and begin by painting. Walk around your motif two or three times and decide *what quality* it is that made you wish to paint it, then find the spot from which your motif best lends itself to your needs and arrange it accordingly. I have drawn the "same motif" in four different conceptions. (Diagrams 13, 14, 15 and 16.) All are as decorative as I could make them and

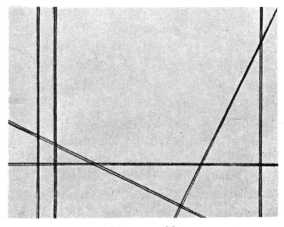

Diagram 11

each has a distinctly different appeal from the others, excepting No. 16, which is *not arranged*. All things in it are of *equal* interest and are therefore stupid.

All these suggestions seem trivial enough, yet I have found, in my years of teaching, very few students who instinctively understood them. Try to feel that each motif you see has about a thousand different possibilities and that you are there to produce the best one.

If your interest centers in certain forms and colors of a foreground, such as groups of flowers of different kinds, certain arrangements and colors of stones and grass; flowering shrubs, or mere contour (or roll) of a simple foreground, the most natural arrangement of your masses will be Diagram No. 12, giving the prominence in size and color to the foreground.

If your interest is in a "sky effect," the predominance of space will naturally be allotted to it. Or if in a sky-and-mountain mood, the space-arrangement of Diagram No. 13 might answer.

If interest centers in tree-groups or tree-formations the arrangement of the spaces shown in Diagram No. 14 will probably approximate the idea.

Diagram No. 15 shows an arrangement of the *buildings,* an "intimate" study. Students generally find this type of motif difficult to arrange, the secret trouble being that they get too much—"all outdoors"—into it. You will note that at the left center of Diagram No. 15 I have laid a sheet out on the grass to bring the house into relation with the ground and to "decorate" that portion of the canvas. Students are always asking how to handle a motif of this kind. Their "handling" is good enough for a masterpiece —except that their arrangement of the masses of subject matter is apt to resemble Diagram No. 16. Here is a real "just-as-I-found-it" kind of motif—indeed, it looks as if they had tried to get into the picture an "all-over" interest, and had succeeded.

This is because the student did not feel or select anything from the potpourri of material. For the same reason (or lack of reason) he may choose a too-distant point of observation (if he wants an intimate picture). Neither the houses nor the mountain, the trees nor the ground, emphasize any "idea" back of the choice (in Diagram No. 16), for *all* are clamoring for attention with equal voice. The composition is neither intimate nor impersonal, but merely a copy of all the things seen exactly as they are. Also note the parallel lines (Diagram No. 16), which do not assist the eye in "getting into" the picture, but do rather cut the picture into oblong, semi-geometric shapes: ground, sky, houses, trees. The composition has no "return line," that is, all forms run parallel and away and have nothing to do with one another. In fact, they give a sliding-by feeling to the composition such as one gets from looking out from the windows of a fast express train. It lacks true composition or creative arrangement. The mere sticking of things on a canvas until it looks like a scene-shifter's work is not composition. Even a mural decoration that requires rectangular architecturally-constructed lines must be tied together ultimately with ameliorating parabolic sweeps so as to unite the otherwise too segregated masses into a dynamic whole.

You will note that while I laid down no rules for the division of your canvas into different areas, I stressed the idea of composing for *one* element or *another*. Obviously, if one does so, the "variety of sizes and kinds of shapes" will come of itself, and a more or less decorative thing will result.

→

Here are five drawings made from the same spot. Diagram 12 shows the ground to the artist's left. Diagram 13 emphasizes the sky effect. Diagram 14 makes the trees prominent. Diagram 15 shows the buildings more intimately. Diagram 16 is unplanned.

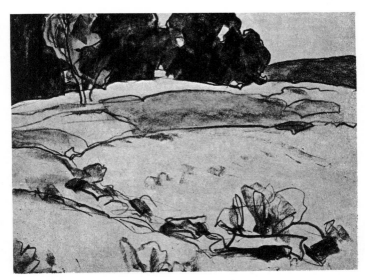

Diagram 12

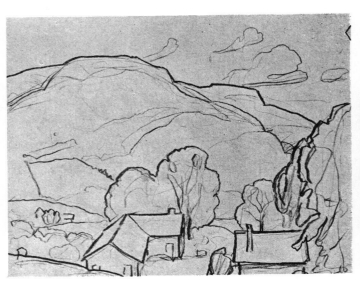

Diagram 13

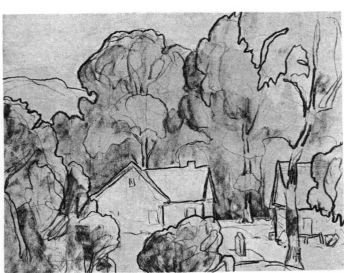

Diagram 14

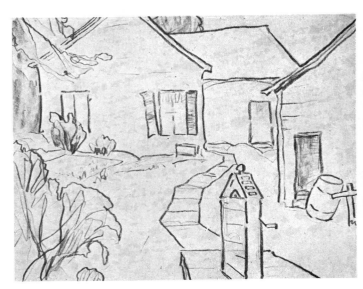

Diagram 15

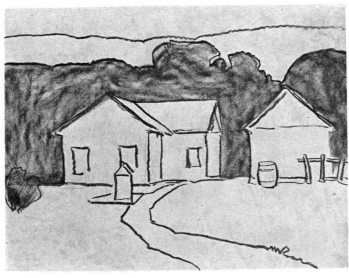

Diagram 16

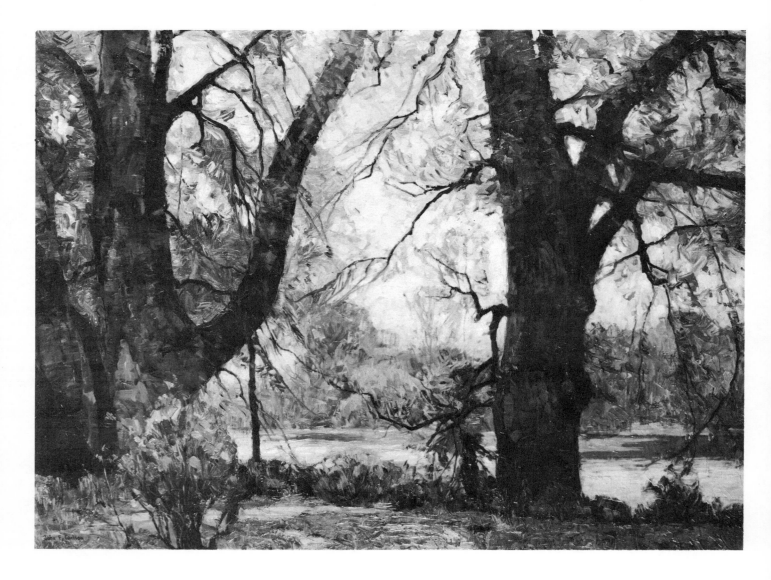

When you find, as here, two trees near together, one "lacy" and the other with thick foliage, you can observe the following: First, the trees when looked at with half-closed eyes will be seen to be of different value, as masses; the lacy tree will be much lighter in value than the solid tree. The main trunk of the lacy tree will be the only real dark in it. The rest of the lacy traceries will be more or less eaten up by the light; in other words, this tree admits enough light through it to lessen its darks, and to take out much of its local color, especially where it meets the sky. The tree with the solid foliage will retain most of its dark value and most of its local color, and its trunk will be considerably darker than the lacy tree's trunk.

5. LIGHT

Unity of Tone and the Meeting of Edges

We shall treat light in this chapter only from the point of view of a visible phenomenon; that is, what it does or how it acts in the painter's out-of-doors, producing color and "atmosphere." Light itself seems to be a thing apart from color and form, although it is the cause of both.

When we speak of light we mean that enveloping, radiating, diffusing something that transmutes our everyday world into a livable and beautiful place.

The artist feels the almost omnipresent light saturating all tones, bringing them into unity, no matter what differences may exist in the "local color" of his masses. This is the true meaning of "tonality"—not a darkening down of colors into a smear.

When men speak of creating "space" in a picture it means only that they have understood their light pretty well. A space in a picture is composed of light. Our eyes do not see black void.

Since actual light cannot be created in a picture, a picture at best reflects reduced daylight (or gallery light, since we do not usually show pictures in the open). We must utilize our limited means (the range of *paints* from white to black) so that we create an illusion or impression of light (and color) over the created forms upon the flat surface of the canvas.

The light creates the local color or colors in any object, because each object possesses certain chemical properties or qualities which absorb some rays and reflect others. The ratio of absorption and reflection determines the color of the object.

After this, it is the form and the texture of the object that, in its withdrawing and projections to or from the light, enhance the beauty of such local color. In nature, light makes form and color visible. In a picture, color creates the form with its variations, by gradations and nuances upon the flat surface of the canvas.

The color of any object depends for its beauty upon the *play of light upon form,* aside from any actual variations in its own or local color. (In contrast, I venture to say that a flat color upon a flat surface, with the light evenly distributed upon it, is seldom beautiful. To beautify such a flat mass we add one or more other flat-color masses of different color in juxtaposition to it, which provides a "harmonious variety," such as we find in posters.) Form or movement of a surface causes these varieties of color to appear, and beauty results.

Besides this, the light's color-cast diffuses itself over and into the colors of such an object and thereby establishes a kind of unity or "tone" over the whole. Thus, there is a vast difference between a group of colors seen under yellowish light, and the same group seen under bluish light, or between the same group seen by moonlight—the latter not only being for the most part greenish in cast but also very reduced in degree of light.

To experiment with this principle, take a white piece of cloth and a brilliantly colored piece and lay them out on the grass where you can study them under different light conditions: sunlight, grey day, moonlight, twilight. The tone of the white piece will be more easily noticed, but you may be sure that the changes that affect the white are also present in the brilliant color, but seen with greater difficulty. Much will be gained through this study. It makes no difference what kind of art work you are employed in doing; the study will sensitize your "color-eye."

After understanding all this, how absurd appear all the attempts that have been made to "catalogue" the color of trees or stones or hills when every varying mood of nature throws the whole into an entirely new scheme of color, and since the degree of change in each color-mass depends upon the color of the light cast upon it. Blue will change under a reddish light more speedily than will red when exposed to the same light. The very joy of color rests upon this evanescence. No one can tell another person *exactly* what the color of anything is, because each of us has a variously differing "color-sense."

There was once a student who, in ardent anxiety to "get the exact color" of certain tree trunks he was painting out-of-doors, actually took his palette up to the trees, and, mixing a daub of color, "tried it" on the bark. Of course, the results of this experiment were unsuccessful, for the student had forgotten that the trees were fifty yards away in nature, and therefore, seen through that much atmosphere. He forgot also that the sunlight shone on the tree trunk *and* on his "matched" daub, which, when seen *upon his picture* under tempered indoor light, was neither exact nor beautiful. We do not paint "exact" colors; we paint them as they impress us, differently every day.

With the painter, the local color has very few thrills. Almost anyone can see local color. It is in the bright light or in the deep shadows, and the transitions between these, that the painter finds interest. Here he has to use all his analytic senses, together with his sight, to find their component parts.

Too vague a color-cast, too undetermined a value, and the desired unity is threatened, perhaps even the form annihilated. It is this searching that makes painting an exciting thing! No stereotyped formulas of color or composition help very much.

Hold up a lead pencil against the sun: the pencil almost vanishes. Look at that green tree—if you walk around it so as to place it between yourself and the sun, the "green" is no longer there as green! Anyone who has been present in a sunlit room during sweeping hours has probably noticed how the sunlight, lighting up the dust near the window, forms a path of gold through the dust-cloud. In seeing the edges of the window and adjacent wall through such a dust-cloud, notice that the dark frame and adjacent walls lighten from an actual dark to a golden dark, and that this golden dust-screen grows darker as it recedes from the window into the corners of the room.

The atmosphere out-of-doors is just such a dust-cloud, only of lesser density, being composed of particles of moisture suspended in the air (the quantity depending upon the meteorological conditions). A dark mass seen at some distance, through this air, is more or less lightened according to the day and the time of day. Especially is this noticeable when looking toward the light (as in the case of the window). Especially, too, is such a mass lightened at the edges touching the sky or light. The power of the dark mass lessens as it approaches the light and becomes simplified into a mass, because the eye cannot readily look into it when the light shines into the eye. It actually seems darker to the eye of the beginner, but if he paints it that way (darker), the light mass (sky) touching it, while being itself a light value, will not seem to give off light rays.

This lack of light is easily noticed if you try to paint a dark tree *too* dark against a brilliantly lighted sky. Your sky may be brilliant yellow or very light blue (or any

Carlson's Guide to Landscape Painting

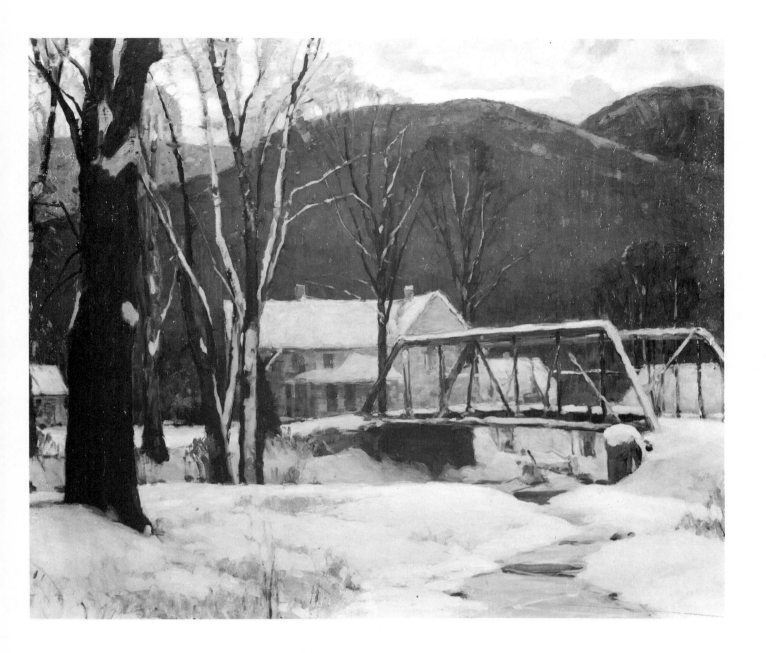

The highest light possible in a painting is white paint, seen in the tempered light of a studio or gallery. Nature's light is the sun. Paint *absorbs* light; the sun gives it. The painter has only reflected light and lighted darks to work with. Therefore, the illusion of space, form, color, light, atmosphere and tone must be painted with some understanding of our limitations. We "see" light as we see color and form, almost as tangibly. Difficult to see, this painting of the light as the unifying agent requires patience and thought.

other light color), but with your too-dark tree painted against it, it will *not* appear to radiate light. It becomes just black paint against light paint, but not *light*. The light not only lightens and simplifies such a tree, but seems to wrap itself *around* the edges in relief against it so that these, more than ever, lose their local color and much of their local value. The more delicate the twig that may come against such a sky, the more the light has power to eat up its value and color. Such a twig becomes at last only a light grey with a modicum of local color in it. With this phenomenon understood, your sky will appear to give off light. If not, it remains a field of color that does not function. It might almost be given as a "recipe" that the smaller the dark mass presented against a light, the lighter and fainter becomes that dark. (If you can remember this when you are drawing a bare tree against a sky, your tree will have less the look of being pasted on the sky.)

As another example of this phenomenon, let us again select a window for our study, preferably a window that has mullions or cross-divisions of varying widths. When looking (with semi-closed eyes) through such a window into the light of outdoors it will be found that the narrower and smaller the mullion the lighter will be its value. (See Diagram C.) Transfer this experiment to the out-of-doors and you will discover the same phenomenon in the value-relations between trunk, branch and twig in a tree (if viewed against the mass of the sky). The smaller the twig the lighter the value of it. At last, only the biggest limbs or the trunk of the tree remain dark. This value-transition from the darker (and bigger) trunk to the outer extreme twigs or edge of such a mass is slow but sure. The light will gradually *over-flow* the lessening twigs, until the tree, which might be a generous dark in its middle part, will, while rising *into* the light, gradually become a light value of grey, tempered with the colors of sky and tree.

Yet at no time does it blend into the sky, but remains a dark tree with a firm edge or boundary line against the sky, much the same as the window retained its square shape in the dust. The proper consideration paid to this truth helps to place a dark mass in a landscape that will "live" in the general enveloping key or color tone. It is, therefore, apparent that while great intensity of color juxtaposition has a place in a landscape, it should not prevail at the expense of this unifying "envelope," if such colors become fainter when approaching a strong light, especially when looking toward the sun. Put as much color in a picture as is compatible with the *kind* and degree of light that you are doing, for there is almost as much "expression" in the general key of your picture as there is in your line or mass or color scheme.

Not only are the value and color-transitions present in a tree when seen against the light of the sky, but also in any dark whatsoever that is placed against any light whatsoever. The only difference is in degree of transition according to the intensity of the light mass against which it is placed (even in a head against a light background in the studio). This halation or diffraction which suffuses light *over* dark masses is not alone responsible for the loss of color and value against the light. The light predominates at the expense of color. The eye cannot see distinctions when looking into the light.

The blue of the sky when approaching the sun becomes a mere colorless glare, while the sky opposite the sun can be viewed with ease, and is blue. The same diffraction of light in that quarter is, therefore, less pronounced and more difficult to see. Using two opposite poles of the sky as a starting point, it will be easy for the student to see that the sky must gradually change or "grade" toward the sun from the point farthest away from it. This can be observed by turning around slowly and observing the sky in all points of this half-circle.

Lateral or "side gradation" is consequently present in the sky (in every quarter of the sky), changing its color every inch, so to speak, except at the point opposite the sun. Even at high noon in summer when the sun is almost, but not *quite,* overhead, the sky toward the north is darker than that toward the south (in our northern hemisphere). This "lateral gradation" of light and color takes place because there is no such thing as flat tone in all outdoor nature—it is changing toward or from the light. Even on a dark, cloudy day the cloud lining nearest the sun is, obviously enough, most brilliant in light.

We have seen now how the light in its aggressive positiveness flows over and around, penetrates all objects and atmospheric particles in its path, even insinuates itself into and *across* shadows and cavities, making these luminous and colorful instead of dead black. (It is the prerogative of the artist to really see light and color, especially in shadows.) To the average layman, light and color do not exist to such exalted degrees. Often we hear persons calling a cloud shadow "black" that to the artist is the loveliest violet-blue. The young artist is somewhat inclined to fall into the opposite error. He is apt to see brilliant colors as much lighter in value than they really are, forgetting that the light on a white object, a cloud, or a white house is lighter than the light on the rich yellow goldenrod (hence he gets some too-light foregrounds that rob the sky of its light and therefore look thin and brittle).

We will now consider in what measure the light is checked or hindered by adjacent and interposing darks. If one were to hold up a piece of dark mosquito netting against a light surface (the sky) it would be noticed that when viewed from a distance of fifteen feet the actual warp and woof of the netting is not visible, but instead, the whole piece

looks like a flat light-grey mass, darker as a whole than the sky. This is caused by a combination of the phenomenon mentioned above, that of the darks losing their intensity when put against a light and the new phenomenon of the light *losing its brilliance when filtered* through a dark mass.

We shall now consider the light of the sky as it touches the edge of the trees, or comes through it in more or less different-sized "holes." These holes vary in value according to their *size* and the consequent amount of light they admit through them. Logically enough, the smaller the "hole," the less quantity of light admitted; therefore, the smaller the hole, the darker or greyer it is in value. The lightest holes through our trees are, then, the largest holes. These largest holes are usually those very important to the structural quality of the tree, because they separate the large foliage groups of the tree from one another. Being the lightest value, they therefore give much of the simple design or pattern of the entire tree.

What was said about the sky-holes through the tree applies in the same manner to all the indentations of the tree's outside edge. They are light or dark, according to their size. Hardly any hole through any tree can be as light as the main body of the sky, for even the largest hole has a lesser quantity of light coming through it than the open sky around the tree. You will soon see that what applies to these holes through a tree applies to every light mass as it varies in size. A church steeple tapering upwards (if white) will slightly darken (if against a dark mass of trees or mountains) because of the diminishing size as it tapers, as will the acute angles of a white house. These are "softened" at the angles for the same reason. Speaking of softening: do *not* soften anything, especially edges. Paint them firm, but with the proper understanding, and they will then "look right." Try to understand the foregoing and you will not regret it.

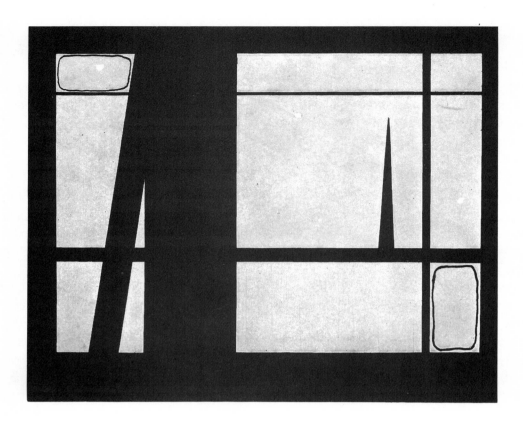

Diagram C

If you have no available trees around upon which to study the "sky-hole" idea, get a piece of *dark* cardboard, 8 by 10 inches, and cut several holes through it, all of different size and shape, ranging in size from one-eighth of an inch to one inch. The holes can represent sky-holes in the tree; they will vary in value according to size. The strips of cardboard left between the holes represent the trunks and branches of our tree. Note how the wide strips are the darkest and vice versa.

In the special Diagram C I have tried to give some of the principal phases of diffractional phenomena. Look at this diagram with half-closed eyes from a distance of three or four feet and note the following:

How the black strips lighten in value in accordance with the decrease of their width or bulk.

How the black steeple-shaped piece grades to a lighter value as it diminishes in size.

How the white areas increase in whiteness according to the increase of their sizes.

How the white steeple-shaped piece grows darker in value as its bulk diminishes.

How the pooling of some white shapes seems to "soften" their edges. All the strips are the same black ink.

The light not only loses its brilliance when it is filtered through a dark mass (such as our netting or the light traceries of a tree), but it even loses a trifle of its brilliance when merely nearing a dark or semi-dark mass. Consider a dark tree against the sky. The sky is a light mass; the *bulk* of the sky is not near the tree, but away from it. The light at the point of contact is *not* reinforced by the main light. This modification of the light near a dark, called *diffraction*, must be so gently accomplished in painting as to be invisible to the uninitiated, who will see that your sky is lighter near your tree (just as nature "appears"). This phenomenon, diffraction, is defined in Webster's as "a modification which light undergoes in passing by the edges of opaque bodies or through narrow slits . . ."

To reiterate, as dark masses approach a light mass they grow *slightly lighter* and simpler. As a light mass approaches a dark mass it grows slightly darker (near the dark mass), but the edge or juncture of the two masses must be firmly held (clear and hard, if you will). In other words, the juncture must be understood and painted, not blurred. If properly painted and understood, the edges will look "atmospheric" in spite of their sharpness or firmness, and what is more, the sky in your picture will even look just as light near your dark masses as at any other place away from them (as it does in nature). If you paint the meeting of light and dark as a beginner would; that is, the light lightest near the dark, and the dark darkest near the light, your sky will not vault back over the landscape, but will hang over in front of the trees, or other dark masses, and the trees will seem to topple forward. In other words, the contrast of value at the edges, being too great, causes that portion to come forward.

I have often been asked by some student to "paint a tree." Students do not realize that if they could "see" a hundred trees painted it would not benefit them unless they understood the "why" of every touch.

What is true about a beginner's landscape is true of his portrait-studies as well. A light face against a dark background seems very light to him, especially at the edge, and the background looks dark, especially near the face. If he could but "snatch" the background suddenly away and replace it with a white one, it would be seen that the edge which looked so light against the dark background is really much darker than the *light* on the face. It is the same with the dark background when painted

with understanding. And remember that the dark background is much reduced in its darkness by its approach to the light face.

Probably the greatest exponent of diffraction, or the understanding of edges, was Vermeer. It will pay the student to study with what care he painted a piece of white paper lying upon the floor ("Woman Reading a Letter").

The highest light possible in a painting is only white paint (and seen in the tempered light of a studio or gallery). Nature's light is the sun. Paint *absorbs* light; the sun *gives* it. The painter has only reflected light and lighted darks to work with (for even his darkest darks in a picture have to have light thrown on them to be seen). His lightest light is somewhere near white paint, which (also in a gallery) has the indoor modified light to show it up.

So far we have studied the value-diffraction only; that is, have studied to see how the masses behaved when their juncture took place relative to their lightening or darkening. We shall now try to see how the *masses as color* behave in such juncture.

First, you may observe sometime, with half-closed eyes, how a telegraph pole (about 30 feet away) seen against a sunset sky will partake across its darkness of the cast or hue of the color in the sky against which it is seen or relieved. The red at the horizon will carry across that portion of the pole seen against it, making it a deep wine color; the yellow zone of the sky will carry across and make the pole against it seem a dark green; the top of the pole will come against the sky above the sunset and it will become a cold bluish dark; and this color-variation is delicate and obscure for the unobserving. The value of the pole will remain a strong dark against the sky (though really changing a trifle in value).

Of course, this phenomenon will not be observed as happening in the case of a *large* dark mass. In such a mass this color diffraction will only be seen at the edge of the mass. The mass is large enough to hold its own, at least in its center, whereas the telegraph pole was so slight a hindrance to the light's passage that it became sympathetically colored. The eye of the observer, could not, in the case of the pole, readjust itself within so small a mass, but was dominated by the colors of the larger light of the sky. The complementary color in the pole was therefore *lacking,* whereas, in the larger masses interposed against the sky, there would be seen a certain presence of the complementary (away from the edges of the mass).

The above example of the pole is an inartistic one, but if once observed will be of help in solving other, more complex color halations. These backwashes of both value and color *do* exist in almost every meeting of color masses and value contrasts, you may rest assured, even in indoor painting, where the source of light is modified. I have called it "sympathetic color-meeting," for want of a better name; others call it "transition." I have seen men who dispensed with it entirely, but I believe that their work has suffered a loss greater than they appreciate. Illustrators are sometimes forced to disregard it, for they are asked to deliver something "contrasty" for the sake of its reproductive qualities.

This theory of halation, if carried to too obvious an exposition, causes a flabby appearance of the masses; if ignored, the masses are static and untied. I remember painting a moonlight picture once that had a red barn in it in relief against a hill in the background which was of a mysterious blue-green color and slightly darker than the barn. I found that, far beyond my anticipation, I had to modify the blue-green hill with red near the barn, making it slightly purplish-grey, before I could make the two masses meet in that light. Not only this, but I had to introduce a minute amount of greenish blue into the red barn where it met the hillside. To do this so that it was

not obviously seen in the picture was not an easy matter. Aside from making the two masses "meet" in the light mentioned, the modulation of the color masses described had the added value of beautifying the two colors.

There is another curious thing that takes place in the juncture of masses, and that is a visible *rounding off* of sharp corners or angles (as was noticed in our church spires). When a mass projects an acute angle into any other mass of differing color and value, the mass into which it is projected seems to *overcome* it with its own color and value. Or in other words, when a mass projects an acute angle into another mass there is a lessening of that acute mass force in its progress, a gradual loss of its extreme conditions. This is but slightly present in the middle register of value contrast, but easily visible in close value-relations (as in moonlight) or in very great value-relations (as in the case of a cedar tree against a brilliant sky, or in the sky projecting an acute angle into a dark mass of trees).

In the moonlight the presence of excessive diffraction is caused not so much by the actual physical halation or spreading of light over adjacent darks, but by the suppression of light masses projected into the darks—acute angles—and also by the fact that the source of light is very much reduced or half-dark and the eye cannot probe into the exact meeting of the edges, but can only accept the large differences, or can only see the big shapes, and these without definite edges. A mountain at night might present a simple straight line against the sky. We can see the sky and we can see the mountain, but any attempt to locate the exact edge or meeting place seems impossible.

A sun ray passing through a square or angular aperture and falling as a spot upon a plane near it will get *more round* as the plane is withdrawn from the aperture until no angles are visible. Of course, a portion of this rounding or softening of such a spot is caused by what is called "penumbra" (in inverse form here) in astronomy. Also, the sun spot has a tendency to round, owing to the hole forming a kind of atmospheric lens which focuses the rays upon the object and which allows the sun to enforce its own shape (round). I have been told that in an eclipse such a sunspot (filtered through a dark mass) will alter its shape upon the surface which it strikes as the eclipse progresses, going through the phases from full to crescent sun and back again. Whatever the cause, the effect is observable and cannot be consciously or unconsciously ignored.

You will see this rounding and softening of far-cast shadows if you study the shadows from any given trunk (in the woods) as it is cast upon nearer or farther tree trunks. The farther a cast shadow has to travel the softer or rounder will its shape become. In like ratio it will also become lighter as it recedes from the object casting it, for reasons given.

Concerning the "complementary colors in shadows," that one hears and sees so much of among beginners, little need be said excepting this: If you see the complementary color anywhere, paint it as you see it, but do not try to invent complementary juxtapositions. It is a visual fact that on occasions when the eye is steeped in or has been subjected to a protracted display of *any one color* it craves the presence of the other two colors combined into a "complementary," to fill the triad, as it were. (See the chapter on Color.) Interesting experiments with this principle can be carried on. Even when you see very obvious illustrations of this phenomenon, as when, for instance, the setting sun diffuses an orange-yellow light over the landscape, and all shadows cast seem to be of purple hue, do not *over*accentuate this quality. Rather remember that you are seeing these purples of shadows through a film of orange-yellow light. This will help you to keep the shadows from being altogether too purple, to which exaggeration you might be sacrificing the entire idea of the landscape. For the timbre of the light permeates all things out-of-doors, even (though slightly) your purple shadows.

The smaller the opening through which the light must pass (be it sunlight, or a light sky, or snow showing through a darker mass) the lower will be the brilliance of that light!

If you can remember this principle when painting a tree or any other mass whatever, you will be surprised at the simplicity of that otherwise over-detailed mass. Instead of calling this chapter "Light," I could as easily have called it "The Proper Painting of Edges," for it is in the meeting of edges that we are really concerned. Anyone can paint a fairly good value-mass or two, but their juncture is a thing requiring thought.

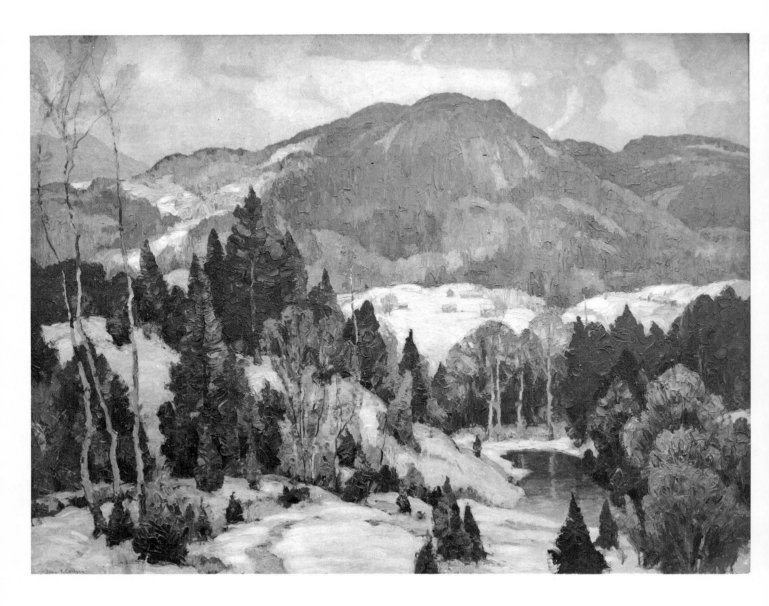

All things become cooler in color and lighter in value as they recede into the distance. Our nearer hills of warm violet will therefore be the darker, and the farthest one of pure blue will be the lightest. Remember that you cannot paint the color of any of the hills or of anything else until you get its proper value.

6. AERIAL PERSPECTIVE
Transitions in Value and Color

After having so strongly insisted upon a "flat poster-like pattern of values" in an earlier chapter, it will seem paradoxical to say here that *there is no such thing as a perfectly flat mass* in all nature! Yet that is exactly what we propose to do. There is method in this madness.

Every angle or plane of an element, flat-lying, upright, arching or slanting, has within its "flatness" marvelous and subtle variations of both *color and value*. A color mass becomes beautiful only when it partakes of these changes. Consider a plaster wall painted by Vermeer, how it flows from window to recess, from floor to ceiling, even though the local color or general tone of the wall might be called "just a grey."

In this chapter we are concerned with aerial perspective, the expression of space by changes and gradations of color distinctness and hue. The first fact is that the hue, shade, or cast of any color mass *is* separable from its weight or value. I have, let us say, three skeins of colored worsted, all of them an olive green, but differing in *value* of olive green, to wit: light olive green, medium olive green, and dark olive green. In other words, these skeins differ only in value and not in color.

I have three other skeins: one a medium-dark green, another a medium-dark red and another a medium-dark purple; these skeins differ only in hue, but not in value.

And I have three other skeins: one a light green, another a medium-dark red and another a dark purple; these skeins differ in value *and* hue.

A value-and-hue transition would be an instance of the medium-dark red blending gradually into the dark purple.

A value transition is most obvious in the blending of the light olive green into the dark olive green.

Having now a firm idea about the difference between *value* and *color* gradations, let us take up each plane or element in its turn and try to analyze just what is taking place within these masses as they recede from the eye. This is to be our prime means of creating a sense of space and air in an otherwise two-dimensional canvas. This is our third dimension.

There is one rule governing color gradations, and that is: all colors become *cooler* as they recede from the eye, except white.

A cool color is one that has a preponderance of blue in its makeup; pure blue being, of course, the coldest.

A warm color is one made up of yellows and reds. There is some discussion as to which is warmest—strong yellow or bright red. I feel that a strong orange (yellow and red mixed) is the warmest.

A blue can be warmed by the addition of yellow or red (or both). The blue in that case becomes either a greenish-blue or a violet-blue, both warmer than pure blue. Yellow can both be cooled and modified by the addition of blue, or by blue and a modicum of red (which make a violet). Red can be cooled by the addition of blue or by blue and yellow (which make a bluish-green). The addition of white to any of these colors or mixtures tends to cool them.

(In these remarks we are dealing entirely with the mixture of pigments and not colored light.)

One of the most important truths bearing upon receding color out-of-doors is this: It is the *yellow* that fades out of a landscape as it recedes from the foreground. This means not only yellow itself, but the yellow in all mixtures, such as brown, warm red, orange, etc. Our green, for example, will range from a sappy yellow-green in the foreground to quite a cool green in the middle distance and gradually diminish in its yellowness as it goes farther back, until it turns to a faint emerald in the distance; and this emerald will become a faint greenish-blue at the horizon. Again, it is the yellow that fades out of receding planes. As the yellow fades out, the violets and blues seem to increase in intensity.

Given a great stretch of country to study this phenomenon, it will be seen that even the violets (purples) eventually give way to the blue. We may have a range of hills, one behind the other; the nearest one may be a warm violet (or contain red, blue, and a slight amount of yellow in its color composition); the next hill behind it will be a *trifle bluer* violet; the next behind it still bluer, and the farthest one almost pure blue (tempered with the prevailing sky color).

So far we have only mentioned the color changes in our stretch of country; let us add another factor: All things become *lighter in value* as they recede from the eye. This makes our law read, "All things become cooler in color and lighter in value as they recede into the distance." Our nearest hill of warm violet would therefore be the darkest, and the farthest one of pure blue would be the lightest.

Remember that you cannot "paint the color" of any of the hills or of anything else until you get its proper value. Let us proceed to inquire a little more into the causes of these gradations. If we understand the cause we will more readily *see* the effect.

The atmosphere is composed of certain gases in which is suspended at all times a greater or lesser number of moisture particles. This moisture may be likened to mist, at one time dense, at another time light. Let us imagine that, instead of the atmosphere being a contiguous whole, it is like a series of very thin films or "curtains" intervening between ourselves and the distant horizon.

Obviously enough, when we observe any *near* object we look through but a small amount of this mist, or a small number of the curtains. These near objects therefore are more sharply defined in outline and richer and darker in color and value. It is well to mention here that the atmosphere itself is apparently colorless. However, when seen in great depths, such as exist between an observer's eye and the visible horizon, it does develop a curious opaquish blue. This bluish hue affects the darks and half-darks in a landscape much more than it affects the lighter tones. Curiously enough, *whites* or *near-whites,* when seen through a great depth of atmosphere, become slightly *warmer and darker* as they recede into the distance. The distant lights or whites cannot, in other words, penetrate the *curtain of atmosphere* to reach the eye with any great brilliance, but are dulled by their interposition. This dulling of the whites as they recede from the eye is best studied in the cloud formations of any fine day.

Science has told us that the atmosphere (about 100 miles high) surrounds our earth in a layer no thicker in proportion to the earth than is the shell to an egg. Outside this layer of atmosphere absolute darkness prevails except for the body of the sun itself, or for any solid or semi-solid body upon which the light rays strike. No "daylight" such as we know it exists out there, for there is nothing to hold or diffuse the light rays. No refraction or diffraction or halation; nothing but a blinding orb of fire on one hand and black shadows on the other; cold, austere, inexorable space.

Carlson's Guide to Landscape Painting

Our atmosphere is the soft receiver and diffuser of light. I spent months trying to make my students see that the sky was seldom as blue as they painted it. The "blue of the sky" is the black void of infinite space beheld through our film of atmosphere. The thicker the film of atmosphere, the less blue the sky appears. When thicker vapors are interposed, as is evident in the case of stratus clouds (heavy, low vapor), the sky becomes a shining silvery mass.

We will begin our study of gradation in the lightest element in a picture, the sky. We will assume that we stand upon a tremendous plain where the sky can be seen in its entire arch. Why does the sky *vary* in color and value in its vaulting from zenith to horizon? (Many people do not know that it *does* vary.)

To answer this question I have drawn lines in radii (Diagram No. 17) from the imaginary observer to the different "degrees" of the arch, or seeming arch, of the sky. It will be readily seen that these lines or radii, in leaving the vertical position and gradually assuming the horizontal, in each degree of removal must travel through *more atmosphere* before reaching the approximate outer void or darkness, and that as the radii lines (or distances through the atmosphere) are lengthened, this outer void becomes more and more veiled as a consequence. The arch of the sky, therefore,

seems to assume a *lighter* and slightly warmer, perhaps greener, cast in its descent toward the horizon.

This gradation or transition of color and value may be said to roughly resemble a large but attenuated rainbow. In other words, it begins at the zenith with its true violet-blue and very gradually assumes a true blue, this blue becoming a green-blue of lighter value than the blue above as it approaches the angle of about 60 degrees (Diagrams Nos. 17 and 18). Note the value gradation of the sky value-zones in Diagram No. 18; from 60 degrees to the horizon, gradually (infinitesimally) a more yellowish green grades down to a roseate hue near the horizon. This roseate hue or rose-grey hue gradually *darkens* when approaching the horizon, where it becomes a thick, warm rosy-grey "haze."

This darkening of the sky a few degrees before it reaches the horizon or ground is one of the most important of all gradations. The discernment of the exact atmospheric conditions of the sky to be painted decides the speed or ratio of all color gradations both in sky and land. The sky is the "key" to the landscape. This darkening, mentioned above, is more readily understood when we appreciate that the densest atmosphere is at the earth's surface, and that any color or light seen through it (along the ground, as it were) has to penetrate a denser veil before

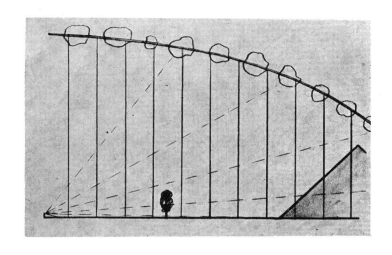

Diagram 17: **The degree of the arch in the pictorial sky. Note that light must travel through more atmosphere near the horizon.**

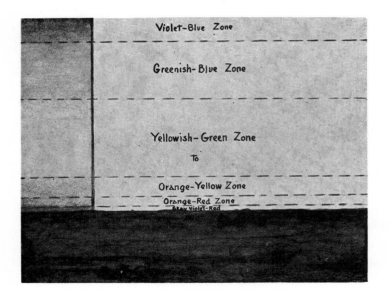

Diagram 18: The gradation of color and value in the sky. Note that this resembles a large rainbow.

reaching the eye of the observer, so dense a veil that it almost casts a shadow. This accounts plausibly for the phenomenon of the sun's turning into an easily-observed *red ball* at the horizon in setting or rising.

The ordinary grey or overcast day presents a quite different problem in its variations and gradations of color and value. In the first place, the value (or weight) of the whole mass of the sky is *lighter* compared to the ground than on a sunny day—a thing that always surprises the uninitiated. To give a logical illustration of this, let us first agree that a white cloud is many times lighter than the blue sky against which it is seen. The usual grey day is a condition in which *many clouds* (and even one or more layers or strata of clouds) entirely cover and obscure the blue sky. But the sun shining upon the upper surfaces of these cloud-strata produces a silvering illumination of these vapors, causing the light to diffuse itself through the vapors before reaching us (in what I have called "sifted" light) and causing the sky to seem a silver white mass in relation to earth. Not only is this arresting and diffusing of the light the *sole* cause why a grey-day sky is lighter than a clear sky, but the very fact of the light's being so diffused, sifted or modified naturally involves a darkening of all the *earth* values,

which by contrast makes the sky seem lighter than it really is.

On a clear day the sun striking the earth with full light raises the value of all earth values, making the sky seem not so light by the lessened contrast.

Clouds on a grey day act as a piece of ground glass in diffusing the light sent through them by the sun and absorbing a great percentage of it in transit. Do not confuse this definition of a grey sky with other grey skies of the more dramatic type, when, for instance, clouds of great density and consequent darkness rush across the firmament. This type of sky produces an ominous merging of earth-and-sky value-relations until all is wrapped in a greenish-blue gloom, or into so-called "black" values.

The color and value gradations of cloud bases vary with the existing atmospheric or meteorological conditions, but in general it can be said that the dark portions or *bases* of a cloud-galaxy, because they come under the head of darks, grow bluer or cooler and lighter as they recede towards the horizon, whereas the cloud "lights" coming under the head of white get a trifle warmer or rosier as they recede. Only one warning before passing on: *Cloud bases,* or the underside of any big cloud, are *very rarely* as dark as the earth-values (such as mountains

Carlson's Guide to Landscape Painting

and trees, etc.), even though they may look so to the beginner. Remember that a cloud is only a more or less dense *vapor* and that a mountain is solid rock. By gaining a sense or feeling of this physical difference much trouble may be avoided.

Leaving the sky with its arching void temporarily, we will observe the plane of earth-values that is most influenced by the sky, namely, the *ground* or flat receding plane. We have said before that all things as they recede from us into the atmosphere become generally lighter and cooler. This truth is very easily observed in the ground plane, and is of more importance in this plane than in any other, because it creates for us the "third dimension" (or depth) in a canvas. The sense of *space,* which is the "biggest form" in a landscape, is worth five times that of any other quality.

This flat ground plane may be composed of multitudinous "color colonies." If we take a flat or semi-flat locality, and study the different fields of a great expanse, we find that no two are alike in color, yet all belong (in value) to the flat plane. There appear fields of green wheat or oats, fallow fields, bare earth, hay fields with patches of sorrel, daisy, "devil's paint-brush" and tall timothy, each with its own characteristic color, and *varying* in weight or value. But *at no time* would their value be as light as the sky nor as dark as the trees (or upright planes). In other words, these color differences *stay on the ground,* and all of them cool as they recede from the eye.

You may find (to your satisfaction) that some distant patch of flowers or a grain field will look very warm or very red. Paint it very warm or very red, by all means; but since you are trying to paint a receding piece of ground in a landscape, rather than the still-life of a patch of flowers in the distance (or the individual field), be sure to make it "stay back" where it belongs, even if you have to resort to stratagem. (In this instance it might mean the painting in

of another patch or field of the same characteristics in the foreground, with much more powerful color than the distant one, to *make* that one stay back.)

This law of diminishing intensity of warm colors as they recede into the distance is a fairly easy thing to see when a big stretch of ground is studied. It is much more difficult to see in smaller masses, such as foreground meadows that terminate in the *near* distance against a grove of trees or group of buildings. It requires much study to discover just how much the color and value of the ground recedes before it reaches the upright plane. To the beginner it does not recede in color or grade at all, and he will paint it without any transition at all—for that reason his field will appear vertical or standing upright, like a wall. The difference *does* exist, and to see it is of great importance.

The change of tone or color caused by the flat plane receding into the atmospheric veil affects *every inch* of the ground to be painted, according to the density of quality of the veils or curtains. The meadow that lies at our feet may be alive with brilliant yellows, greens, reds and warm violets, when the same kind of meadow three miles away may appear as a silvery grey-green with pale pinks and over all a bluish "bloom."

Of course, we have many days with very little of this atmospheric charm. If the air is clear (of very slight vapor particles), we call it a "hard day." A monotone color scheme prevails through lack of atmospheric transitions of color.

Could we look across a fifteen-mile stretch of meadows we would at last reach a horizon (or false horizon) where little or nothing remains of the brilliance of color found at our feet or foreground. Again, if we were now to name the color that had lost most of its identity in this transition from foreground to distance, we would answer "yellow." The yellow fades into practical nothingness long before the other two primary colors. The other two colors remain, al-

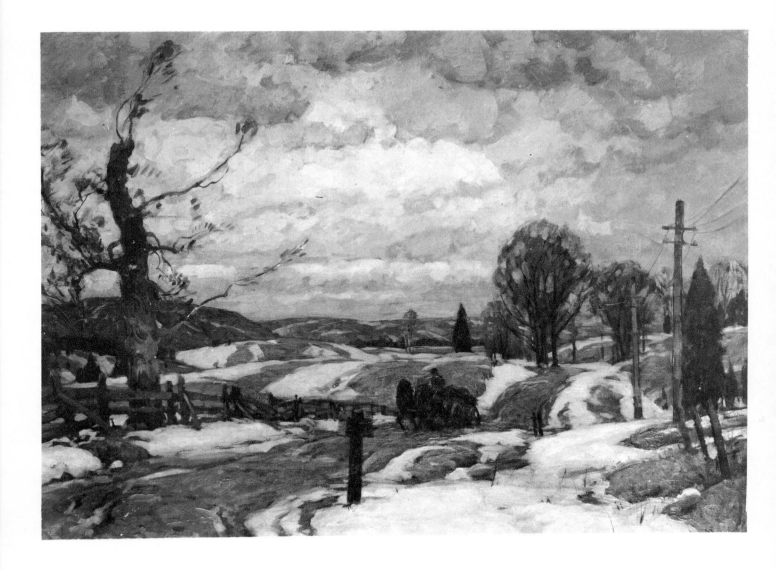

Do not attempt to paint the foreground up to or immediately near your feet, but begin it rather at the point where it is seen when you are looking at the *whole* motif. Otherwise, you will falsify the linear perspective and this will necessitate the employment of terrific detail that will detract from the whole. Leave out the intimate detail you are not conscious of when looking straight ahead on a level line. Corot advised: "Begin your foreground fifty feet away."

though in attenuated state. The red is next to go, and the blue remains.

Of course, no one color can exist "pure" in the out-of-doors without a lesser or greater tempering with the other two, this tempering being decided mostly by the colorcast of the light, with its myriad reflections and refractions. When we speak about the "tone" of any color we mean just that; that it partakes, is tempered by, or is influenced by other colors or by a sharply-colored light. When we speak of a distant mountain being blue, for instance, it does not mean that it is a simon-pure blue—which does not exist, especially out-of-doors! Our blue mountain might be a pale greenish blue (which means that yellow enters into its composition in a minute way) or it may be a pale violet-blue (which means that it partakes to a small degree of red). It may in many instances be a marvelous mixture of yellow, red and blue, with the blue predominating. Thus we get to the unnameable colors, which are the most interesting, after all.

But if the distant mountain is greenish-blue, a nearer hill will be greener, with a trifle of red or violet in its making, and the foreground will be very green. And if the same mountain is of a violet-blue, a nearer hill will be more violet, contain more red than the distant hill, and in this violet will exist a minute portion of yellow, enough to make a delicately warm "toned" violet, at least warmer than the distant hill. This presumes that the mountain and nearer hills are somewhat similar in their actual local color. We might make a converse law regarding this color transition by saying: "One can never paint a distant mountain brilliant yellow and a foreground bright blue, for the mountain would 'come out' and the foreground 'swim away' in proportion to the degree of color 'saturation' in the masses named."

The plane or value-masses that will next attract our attention is the vertical or upright plane. Among the most important objects that comprise this are, of course, the trees. The character and growth of the trees will be treated at length in a subsequent chapter; we shall treat of them here merely as dark *graded* masses. These upright planes, on account of the surface they present to the light (and on account of their generally darker local color), are the darkest objects in a landscape. Infinite variety of color will be found in the component groups or individual trees of this plane: warm green, cold green, russet, violet, red, as well as varieties in their light-and-dark value relations. But even with these differences, and even with the modelling from shadow-to-light upon the individual trees, the mass when seen through half-closed eyes remains a fairly simple dark mass, intact against the sky or ground.

Exceptions to this idea are frequently seen, of course. When the wind blows smartly, the trees in bending often upturn their leaves so that their silvery undersides are presented to the eye, sprinkling the tree with a myriad of starry lights or light reflections on the windward side of the tree. However, the portion of the *inside* of the foliage visible between the starry lights, as well as all the leeward side of the tree, remains dark, the darkest natural object in the landscape. Another exception to the regular rule is found in trees whose foliage has turned yellow in autumn. The beginner, seeing such a tree, is apt to paint it as a mass of light yellow paint. Experience will teach him that even a light yellow tree will have *shadow masses* where the light cannot penetrate, and will also have many parts of the structure of trunk and branches showing, and that these shadow masses and branches *together* are the important structural element that must support the light yellow glare of the sunlit leaves. It is these rich darks *within* the upright plane which still hold to their plane and hinder even yellow trees from becoming mere ghosts of trees.

The tendency in the student is to abuse

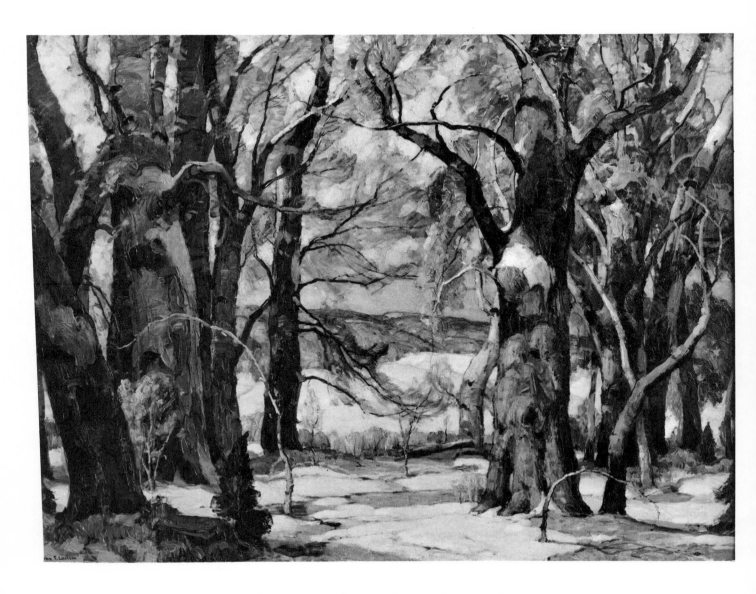

Observe carefully that trees, as they recede into the atmosphere, never lose their identity as upright planes. A tree in the foreground is of positive color (a warm green, let us say). The same tree when viewed from a distant point might be a cool green or even a greenish-blue, depending entirely upon the distance and consequent number of curtains of atmosphere through which it is seen.

the structural angles, all for the sake of "getting the color," as though color could be obtained by reversing a physical truth. If the blue, for instance, of a given sky is painted with such abandon that the sky begins to assume the appearance of cavernous darks and granite ledges, where cavernous darks and granite ledges should not and could not exist, and this sky as a consequence looks "strong" enough to support a cavalry charge (while the poor land, lighter with its pale pinks and warm greens, looks transparent), the painter of such incongruity may be "getting the color" but he is certainly not painting a landscape. What I have called a landscape sense should help prevent such performances.

It has been seen that a flat mass of dark value represents the upright plane in the beginning of a landscape. Whatever local color this mass may possess, or whatever modulations may be necessary within the mass to give it form, these upright masses almost invariably get slightly *lighter* by degrees as they rise from the flat; and not only lighter, but *cooler* in tone. The darkest and warmest portions of these upright masses are usually *near,* but not *at* the ground. There also occurs on a tree a lateral or side-to-side transition of value and color, approaching the source of light.

To illustrate this idea let us assume that the abstract form of all trees *combined* would be a shape something akin to the elongated gas bag of a balloon. The light from the sky falling upon such a shape would result in an increasing darkening of its color as it leaves the lighted area on top. There would also be a lateral gradation of color and value from the side nearest the sun to the side farthest from it. This sounds absurdly simple, but I have found few students who felt this when painting a tree.

This big form is difficult to preserve, because by the time we have modelled the smaller forms upon the big and added the

necessary highlights and shadows, the chances are that we have overdone these so that our big form is cut up and spotty. These highlights and shadows belong there, but we may put *too many* brilliant highlights upon it; meaning that we may put lights upon the upright form that should possibly belong to the flat-lying plane. This passion for putting too many and too brilliant "lights" upon *all* the forms or planes is responsible for more good studies coming to grief than any other cause.

My whole energy is usually necessary to keep beginners from painting the *entire tree* with highlight value. Such a tree looks like an eerie will-of-the-wisp floating in the landscape, instead of the virile, growing, rooted, reaching thing that a tree is.

Before leaving the subject of upright planes, it is imperative that we discuss their color changes as they recede into the distance. We have established the truth that "all colors receding from the eye become cooler and lighter," and that this cooling of color, as it goes into the distance, is easily seen when looking over a wide stretch of country. Obviously enough, if our meadows stretch back and become cooler and lighter, the same thing happens to our upright planes. A tree in the foreground is of positive color (a warm green, let us say). The same tree when viewed from a distant point might be a cool green or even a greenish-blue, depending entirely upon the distance and consequent number of curtains of atmosphere through which it is seen. Especially do the *shadow-portions* of such a distant tree become very cool or blue. A wooded and steeply inclined mountainside in the distance can become very blue in certain lights. I mention this because of the curious fact that the bluing effect of the atmosphere upon *all* things receding into it (or going into the distance) has greater effect upon the *darks* in a landscape than upon the half-darks or half-lights. It will readily be understood, then, why the aerial perspective or cooling of a landscape is more easily seen by the beginner in receding groups of trees than in meadows.

Observe carefully that trees as they recede into the atmosphere or are seen at great distances, *never lose* their identity as upright planes. They have grown lighter and cooler, but still remain *darks* as compared with the surrounding areas or elements (which have, of course, also grown cooler and lighter).

We shall now discuss the third and last element of the earth values, namely, the slanting plane or mountains. This plane partakes of light in a quantity somewhere between the upright and the flat-lying planes. It is, therefore, held here to be a half-dark. All this refers to the average mountain on an average day. The average hill or mountain is composed of various slanting planes, varying in abruptness and undulation (only very rarely rising "sheer").

Because of this slant toward an apex, the base of any hill or mountain is nearer the eye than its outline against the sky. This hill mass or mountain is, first of all, the semi-dark flat mass because of the angle it presents to the sky.

We must now study to make that value recede from the eye (in color) as it rises. Because of its slanting plane, the color of any mountain (as it recedes from the eye) does not grade so swiftly as the flat-lying plane. In other words, between the base and the apex of the mountain there are not so many of our curtains to be traversed. Because of the comparatively slight gradation in any mountain mass, we need to use extra care in its interpretation. The mountain usually *appears* as a flat mass, but we know it is not. (Diagram No. 17.)

Not only this, but as the hill approaches the sky line it recedes more suddenly from the eye in its *rolling-over*. The value is, therefore, suddenly but gently lightened by the sudden recession of plane, and the color, therefore, correspondingly cooled. When this mountain mass has been so understood and painted, the sky value (light) coming against it with its much lighter mass will create an atmospheric edge (without any *softening* of that edge). Then, too, the atmospheric edge is augmented by the fact that the sky is actually darkened slightly by the mountains at that point of contact with it. (See the chapter on Light.) The mountain mass does not roll over in any sausage-like way, but is made up of greater and lesser declivities and rollings, with roots or spurs protruding from the summit to the base. While these must be noted to give the mountains the same amount of form within the mass as is seen at the profile against the sky, the truth nevertheless prevails that all these variations of plane and form gradually ascend with the general slant of the mountain, and these variations of consequent color-differences must therefore be superimposed upon the big receding form. If this can be done, the mountain will retain its apparently flat value mass in the picture and yet look rugged and strong in spite of the necessary details.

Remember, please, that no mountain or slanting plane, be it green or blue or pink or rose-russet, can escape from the law of gradation. The slant of its plane will determine the suddenness and the gradations of color and value.

The local color of objects and even of great masses will sometimes under unusual conditions defy this law of gradation. You may be sure that this condition is but local (and mostly temporary). Once, for example, there had been a tremendous forest fire on one of the distant mountains of our valley. In the spring when the green leaf-buds began to come out, this charred spot remained dead and became a reddish-brown color. The red spot seemed to "stick out" much nearer than the surrounding forest upon the mountain; because of its warm cast it seemed to partake less of the atmosphere usually enveloping so distant an object. The mountain therefore was graded reversely from cool bluish-green at the bottom to a warm russet-purple at the top, of slightly darker value than the green. All was a mere local accident. There are many such instances of accidental reversion of laws and rules in a day's work in the open.

Let us take, for example, a yellow barn adjoining other buildings (a red barn, for instance), with fields abutting. The barn at the corner nearest us might be a pale yellowish-green, might, in its recession toward the point where it joined the red barn, become a hot orange owing to the reflection of the red barn upon the yellow one. We cannot in such an instance positively say that the receding angles of the yellow barn grow cooler, nor, as the modernist would claim in his "building up with color," that the nearest point of the barn would be yellowest, for this would create a formula for all yellow barns regardless of the influences surrounding them, and all yellow barns would be forever alike. In truth, our yellow barn above would be an instance of the *breaking* of the law. Or take the same example applied to a grey barn receding and meeting a yellow barn. The grey barn would again defy the cooling law and become yellower as it receded from the eye. All this, together with the fact that the sky reflection is usually stronger (causing a cooling or bluing) at the top of any tall object (causing an up-and-down transition), makes any dogmatic "rule" absurd.

Suppose the ground surrounding the base of the same yellow barn is rich in brilliant green reflecting back upon the local color of the barn, especially near the ground and under the eaves—what a rich green the barn would become! Or suppose the ground is not green at all, but red with sorrel or white with snow, what different colors the barn would assume! Again, the cooling at the top of the mass may be counteracted and transmuted into something even *more* beautiful by the possibility that the local color

(yellow) of our barn has been affected by its exposure to wind and weather and therefore parts of the surface which have had less exposure (for instance, at the top near the eaves) are of a newer and richer yellow than the main mass (plus the sky reflection). All of these conditions would defy any "color recipe."

This study to see homely instances of what we might call "surprises upon a yellow barn" is only one of many. Every mass, mountain, tree or meadow, comes under like rule-defying influences. Portrait or still life, it is all the same. Consider how our very homely side of a yellow barn has become beautiful and interesting under these variations. It is the mission of the artist to see these beauties and impart something of them to the man who sees not. Therefore, you, a student, should know all you can of laws of gradation and transitions from yellow to violet, but do not swallow any of them whole. Remember that it is the *unexpected* and *unsuspected* color-transitions in any object (caused by the accidental influence of environment) that are *most* beautiful.

Any academic formula, modern or ancient, causes a procession of tiresome repetitions and a preconceiving state of mind that lacks enthusiasm; most of all, it causes a blindness to the miracles taking place before our very eyes.

"Ah," say some, "our yellow barn, treated in direct accordance with your 'accident', will not go back—we will lose the feeling of projected form." Rest assured that, if well "seen" with regard to all other necessary qualities in its rendition (such as the linear construction of its angles and a careful watching of the darks as they recede and grow lighter), the barn, or any other form, will "build up" beautifully and without the obviousness of effort so constantly present in immature work. Once this is appreciated by you, it will definitely separate your work from the mere approximations of a "beginner."

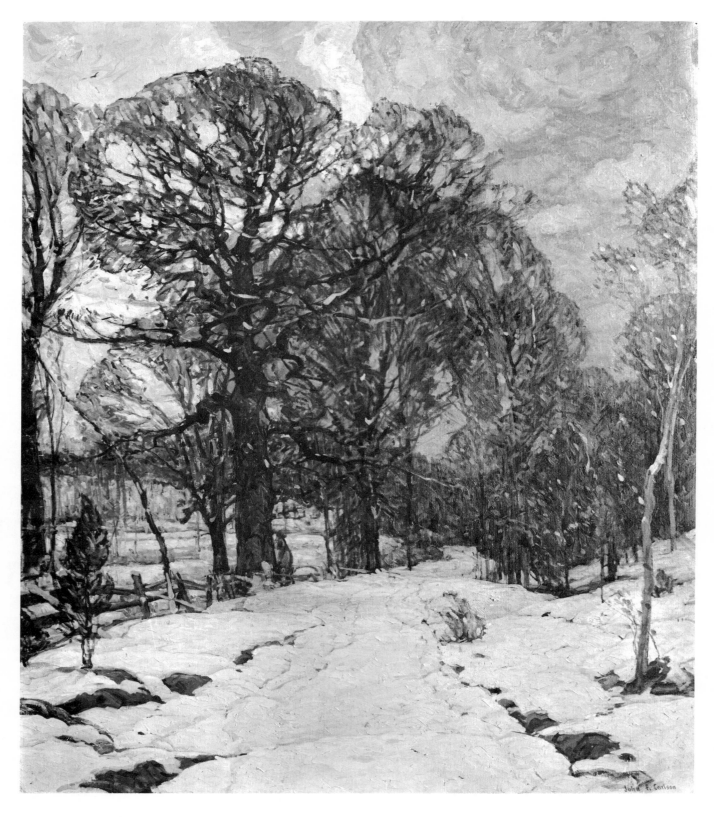

Linear perspective is the basis of the illusion of a "third dimension" or depth in a picture. Note the diminution of the receding forms toward a vanishing point at the real or "accidental" horizon.

7. LINEAR PERSPECTIVE

It is difficult for the beginner to discover linear perspective in a landscape, because of the innumerable vanishing points that an uneven surface like the ground presents. In addition there are many confusing things like light, color, and atmosphere (aerial perspective), so any exact help is usually very welcome to the novice.

Aerial perspective is the *color* diminution toward the horizon. Linear perspective is proportionate diminution of sizes of forms toward the horizon or distance.

For example, almost anyone can see perspective in a geometric form, such as the Flatiron Building, standing upon a flat base. Anyone can see how the lines of the different tiers of windows all converge or come closer together as the building "goes away" into the distance. If this coming together of lines were to continue (in our imagination) to a certain point beyond the building, these lines would eventually converge to one point. This is called the "vanishing point" in linear perspective. Every form or shape that deviates and recedes from the eye (whether vertical or horizontal) partakes of this diminution or perspective.

But it is a difficult thing to see how this law applies to a group of trees or to a piece of ground, although it is as surely present and necessary toward the establishment of the depth in these things as in the Flatiron Building. Especially is it difficult to see linear perspective in a group of trees when, for instance, the smallest trees may be nearest you; especially, too, because these trees are varied in form and not true geometric shapes. The law cannot therefore be applied very easily to them "by rule," but must be *felt*. If we know something about this law in a semi-mechanical sense we can more readily feel it in objects not mechanical. The student should develop a kind of visual perspective, based upon scientific perspective. It might be called "painter's perspective."

As in our buildings, so in trees, sky, ground or mountains: they all converge toward a vanishing point. They are dissimilar to a building in this respect—that their vanishing points can occur almost anywhere, owing to their multitudinous slants or planes, whereas a building, being level and plumb, always has its vanishing point at the horizon. Of course, if we look straight at the square front of a building no recession takes place. We have then merely the vertical and the horizontal "elevation."

All rectangular, level and plumb shapes have their vanishing point at the horizon when they recede from the eye: the shapes occurring above the eye point *down* to the horizon; the shapes occurring below the eye point *up* to the horizon. The horizon always is at eye level. Buildings, barns, houses, etc., are always placed "level," even when built on a hill, and for that reason their vanishing points are always at the horizon. (Diagram No. 19.) Needless to say, these vanishing points can be at any point along the horizon: far to the right or left of your viewpoint, out of your "picture" or view entirely—all according to the acuteness with which your plane recedes.

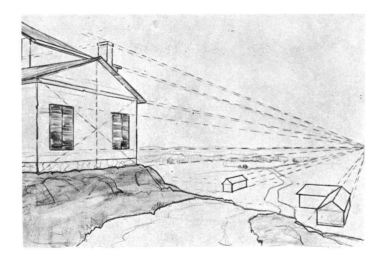

Diagram 19: The most obvious example of perspective is in the projection of buildings. A group of trees of unequal sizes would be under the same influence, but would be less obviously receding from the eye.

Forms such as occur in a landscape are always deviating from the flat plane and their vanishing points are sometimes difficult to feel. These forms are not mechanical or rectilinear, but multiform. They can occur on any plane, from the flat to the vertical. Their vanishing point can truly be said to be "anywhere," as can anything that occurs on the contour of the sloping ground.

In Diagram No. 20, note how the road changes its vanishing point according to the slant traversed, with very sudden diminution on all flat or fast-receding places as in the foreground and top of middle-distance mountain. (Lines running straight into the centre of any view are called "speedy recessions.") Note that the road climbing the steep slant of this mountain diminishes in size but slightly (and has a vanishing point "somewhere in the sky"). Note that this road is continually growing smaller as it recedes from foreground hill to distant horizon. Note the speed with which it traverses these planes. Note that because I am looking *across* the road (at the top of the hill) it becomes suddenly much narrower than the mere receding plane of it would warrant.

If you can apply this to all other things that exist in the above landscape you will have a thorough understanding of landscape perspective. I have placed "average" trees along this road to show that they follow the speed-of-diminution intrinsic in the rolling ground. Note that in the foreground I am looking *along* the ground. I have gotten the "looking down" quality of perspective of the valley just beyond the foreground by considering that I am looking more directly *at* this plane rather than along it, as the degree of diminution partakes of more of the steep slant of the hill than it does of the other planes.

Our next consideration is the linear perspective that we find in the sky (clouds). All lines converge toward the horizon, even those of the sky. Those of the sky converge in a general way downward; those of the ground in a general way upward. I have made the lines in Diagram No. 21 all converge toward one point on the horizon.

On the same principle, because I stand *on* the flat ground and look up *at* the "plane" of the sky (rather than *along* it), the lines of perspective in cloud formations diminish or converge less suddenly than the perspective on the flat earth. Exactly the same thing happened when I was looking *down* into the valley, in an inverted way, in Diagram No. 20. Both instances produced a *less* swiftly receding plane.

The average cloud naturally conforms to the law of receding and consequently diminishing sizes. A cloud may be of any size, anywhere, occasionally, but the majority conform to the diminution described. Only

Carlson's Guide to Landscape Painting

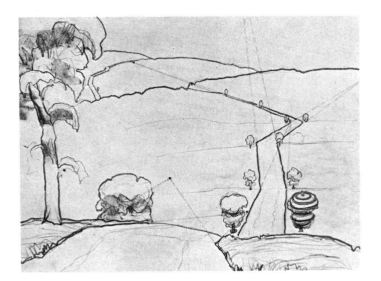

Diagram 20: Changing vanishing points in a twisting road.

understand this, that while a very large cloud *may* hang at the horizon, that same cloud arriving at the zenith would be infinitely larger.

If a mountain or hill should rise in our landscape in such a way as to obstruct our view of the horizon, the arching and receding sky (or clouds) would ignore this temporary "horizon" and proceed back to the *real* horizon (out of our vision, of course) at its own ratio of convergence. It is this *continuance* of the sky back of the mountain, with the clouds coming up over it (and following their *own* perspective), that helps to give a sense of height to the sky and

mountain in our picture, as shown in Diagram No. 22. Of course, we speak of "converging" lines in the sky in only a figurative sense. We can only *feel* these unseen lines.

I said before that there was but little in a landscape to get hold of to establish our perspective. All the more we need to study to make that little absolutely right, so that it may help rather than detract. We have to use ditches, fences, groups of trees, buildings, clouds, clearings, whatever presents itself, to gain our point. Still we must hide this difficulty by using as few of these extra means as possible. Otherwise such means become a detriment to the *expression* of

Diagram 21: Linear perspective in the sky. All lines converge toward the horizon, even those of the clouds and the vault of the sky.

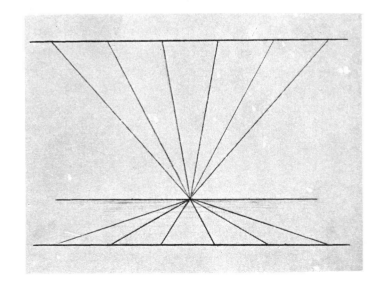

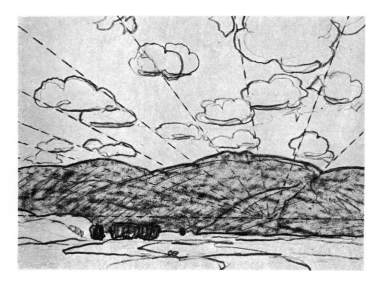

Diagram 22: When a mountain obstructs our view of the horizon, the arching or receding sky ignores this and proceeds back to the real horizon, although it is out of our vision.

the picture, which is the paramount proposition.

A knowledge of perspective gives us more freedom in the handling of our lines in a picture, for we can adapt perspective towards our need of direction in certain lines; and we can do this without any abuse or distortion of such forms.

Perspective, when rightly used, is an auxiliary to a worthy cause; when inartistically used it is only a mathematical equation. A road, because it follows the contours of the ground over which it passes, is (next to trees) the most difficult of any landscape element to draw. The road recedes into the picture in a general diminution, but on account of its lateral turning and twisting, its going up and down, and its gentle side-slants while receding, it presents about all of the elements of perspective and its different vanishing points. In any given road the perspective will be less obvious than in my drawing, on account of the *gentle transition* from one plane or slant to another. A gently undulating road in nature (Diagram No. 20) really *shows up the form* of the ground, which form naturally causes all the elements of the ground, such as patches of fern, colonies of flowers, different colored grasses, fences, clearings on a hillside, etc., to follow its contours. Once having felt a road truly, the student will never again make

the ground in his picture look like a graded flat mass.

A railroad track going across a desert or flat plane points *unerringly* to the horizon, even though it twists and turns laterally (Diagram No. 31), whereas a country road as it meanders up and down upon rolling ground (in wandering towards the horizon) presents a varied number of vanishing points, according to the degree of slant of the hills it traverses. On a very steep hill, for instance, the vanishing point of our road will temporarily be somewhere up in the sky (if the road is running directly into the picture). All this holds, of course, whether applied to a road or a field or clouds.

To illustrate further the complicated perspectives that may occur on an undulating form, I have taken a piece of undulating foreground (Diagram No. 23) and instead of drawing its component details, such as groups of different grasses, stones, flowers (allowing that these detail elements have been arranged in "groups" as suggested elsewhere in this book), have converted all these into *round* disks. These disks conform in their "lie" to the form of the ground. The hoops represent the groups of foreground detail, and *like* these details, though made up of large and small circular hoops, they nevertheless diminish in size as they recede into the distance.

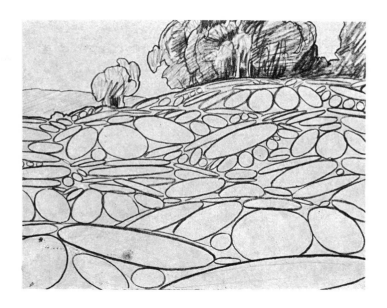

Diagram 23: Semi-circular and curvilinear groups of grasses and rocks, showing how they are affected by perspective and how they behave in their third dimension.

Whether these disks are large or small, they still conform to the differing slants upon which they are thrown, and in a *general way* no matter where they are placed, diminish in size as they go back over this meadow. This is exactly the case with the "incidents" upon the ground (those details which are so muddling to our conception of the big form of the ground). This applies exactly, too, to all forms, on all the elements, in their differing degrees of slant or "movement." It will benefit you greatly to study and apply this analogy of disks or hoops.

The student will, of course, realize by this time that the law of perspective not only affects angular objects, but all shapes and forms. Failure to realize this causes many beginners to draw inclining or flat-lying, roundish forms without any perspective, and consequently all such forms stand upright instead of receding.

Naturally, a circle is equally affected by perspective, but it is more difficult to see it. The geometric way of deciding the exact diminution or flattening of a receding circle is by first computing the recession of a square under the same conditions. This scientific way of proceeding seldom is of real use to the student. The knowledge of it *is*.

In Diagram No. 24, it will be seen that

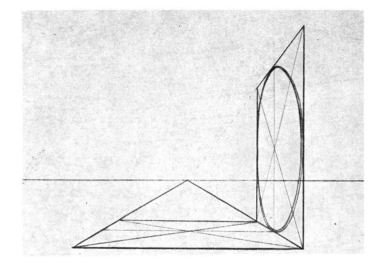

Diagram 24: The effect of perspective upon a circle. It becomes elliptical and flattened out toward the distance until only a mere slit remains.

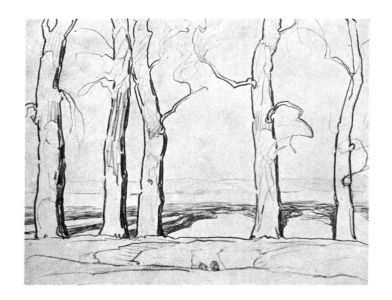

Diagram 25: In perspective, the fullness of contour decreases as cast shadows recede from the eye. At the same time, the shadows follow the form upon which they are cast.

the farther half of the square is smaller than the forward half. When a circle is drawn upon the square (before laying it down), the circle shares the quality of getting smaller when it is laid flat. The forward edges of the circle "bulge out" more than the farther edge, exactly as the square does.

In no way can this be studied to better advantage than in the shadows of trees which are shown (in Diagram No. 25) falling upon a flat plane or field. If this shadow should happen to fall on an undulating or rolling surface, it would, of course, conform to this roll exactly as our disks did, and at the same time (like the circle) become less rounded and more flat-oval as it recedes into the distance.

The lack of linear perspective has the curious effect of dwarfing the heroic object in a landscape painting. A tree that otherwise would look large can be ruined by this lack, that is, made to seem too small and insignificant. A certain proportion of the canvas is allowed, we will say, for a foreground. By understanding perspective we can treat that small space so that it suggests *miles of space.* By a lack of understanding we make it stand upright, like a stone wall. We can make a tree like a toy, or make it look heroic. If a tree looks heroic, the sky back of it will look sublime.

To illustrate this idea I have drawn in Diagrams Nos. 26 and 27 two pictures with similar spaces allowed for foreground, using the identical tree in each. The trees are drawn the *same size,* but they look vastly different in size (which proves that you might fill a whole canvas with a tree and still have it look like a mere plaything). One tree looks near and small; the other farther away and large. In No. 27 I have constructed the foreground in good perspective; in No. 26 I have *ignored* perspective.

In many foregrounds in nature there is little to get hold of for the purposes of perspective construction, but there are always *some things,* such as groups of grasses, flowers, stones, depressions, cloud shadows, tree shadows, paths, roads, etc. If any of these "materials" exist, use them to your purpose—but sparingly. Remember that the less material you use to carry conviction in a picture the better your picture will be. After having learned how to use the materials before you, eliminate and consequently simplify. But unless you have learned how to employ all the means, you can do very little intelligent elimination, because you might eliminate the most necessary "constructives."

An important (nearby) tree in a picture has probably the most obscure perspective

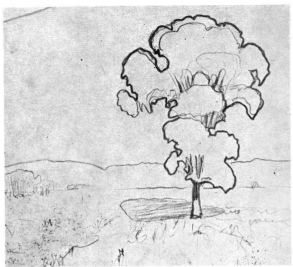

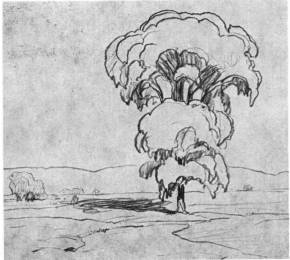

Diagram 26

Diagram 27

of all, but since it is present we must know it. Let us suppose that we were to stretch a gigantic cloth bag over a large tree. Suppose that before so doing we had drawn parallel lines horizontally upon this balloon. After enclosing the tree in this giant bag, it would, when viewed from the ground at a distance of twenty yards, present the appearance shown in Diagram No. 28. It will be noticed that the stripes, instead of remaining horizontal, as they are near the ground, become gradually elliptical or curvilinear as they approach the top of the tree, due to the recession of that plane. The same tree and bag would, when seen from a hill-side or looking *down upon it,* present the reverse appearance (Diagram No. 20).

This quality of perspective in a tree is almost impossible to see while painting, owing to the fact that the various rolling forms of the foliage within the big mass tend to obscure it. But an appreciation of it will help to give height to your tree, and to put it in its proper place. We seem to *look up* at it. Do not worry much about this until you understand all the other qualities of a tree. I drew the examples to help the student feel the presence of perspective in all objects.

An understanding of the decreasing move-

Diagram 28: The most obscure perspective of all is in an important tree in a picture. The stripes that are horizontal near the ground gradually become elliptical as they approach the top of the tree.

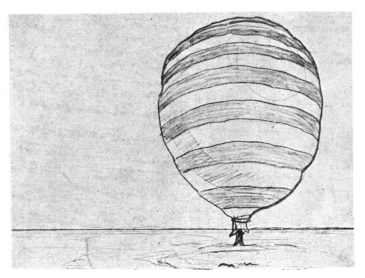

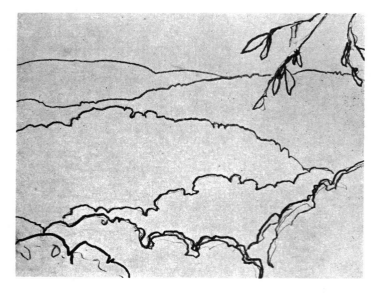

Diagram 29: In overlooking a big valley, first drawing the edges of the big elements helps create the illusion of space. Note the gradually decreasing contour of the big shapes as they recede.

ment of edge details as they recede into the distance is a great asset in creating the idea of space. Knowing that all things go back smaller as they recede from the eye, note the gradually decreasing contour of your big shapes. (Diagram No. 29.) If we were overlooking a big valley, far into the distance, the mere drawing of the edges of the big elements should help us create space. From the farthest mountain edge to the nearest leaf on a tree the progress would be visible.

This does not mean that you must forever be putting your largest shapes foremost, but merely that you should understand the general truth, so that at least any deviation from natural facts will make sense. If a *small* tree is needed as a spot in your composition, in a nearer plane or place than your large trees, it will not hurt your principle of receding sizes at all, if you will make it frankly a small tree in character.

There are instances, when painting from nature, in which it might be well to suppress a physical fact. In a large group of trees (four or five) the arrangement in nature might be such as this: The trees are of various sizes from very large to medium. The smallest tree of all in this group is growing nearest to you; the largest tree is farthest

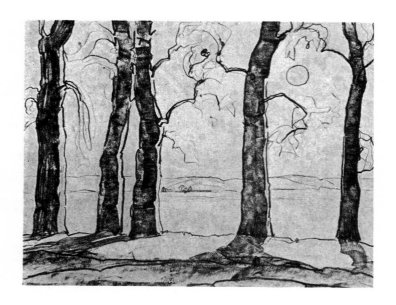

Diagram 30: Shadows coming toward you increase in size, partaking of linear perspective according to the quantity of light and shadow. The disk of the sun shows where the light is coming from, although the lights on the trunks would suffice to do this.

Carlson's Guide to Landscape Painting

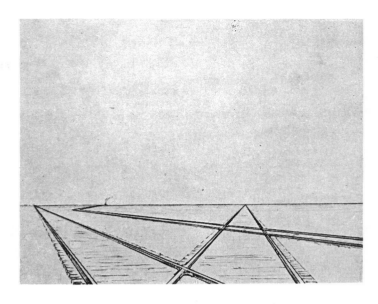

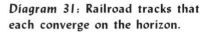

Diagram 31: **Railroad tracks that each converge on the horizon.**

away; the intervening trees are placed in order of their size in inverse perspective between the first named trees, in other words, always increasing in size as they go back. I call this a *local freak*. While the color gradation and value gradation in such a group would, if well painted, put the trees in their proper receding plane, I believe that since it was not *necessary* to select this group from this angle of vision, I would rather walk to the other side of the group and make the trees *help* the idea of perspective space in my picture, unless there are excellent artistic reasons for not doing so.

The farther away the object is, the less the perspective is visible within its mass. The perspective is flattened out, as seen in our disks. In a distant mountain it is less violent, for that reason, than in a nearby tree, though it still prevails in the big forms. The trees that are at the base of the distant mountain have (on account of this distance and consequent diminution in size) no semblance of perspective within their mass. This is because both top and bottom are about level with the eye.

It will be discovered that the larger the picture the less pronounced the perspective that will be necessary, owing to the fact that we look at a large canvas from a greater distance and the objects in the canvas begin

for that reason to partake of middle-distance perspective or are slightly flattened out. There are some painters who evolve a "viewpoint" for their picture, and relatively decide the *degree of perspective* to be used in such a picture. It is best, however, not to become too scientific.

Since all things receding from the eye become smaller, shadows cast upon a flat field, whether they are coming toward you (as is the case when looking in the direction of the sun) or whether going away from you (as when looking directly away from the sun) do nevertheless converge or get smaller as they recede from the eye.

If you could look from a balloon down upon a field lighted by the sun, and trees were in that field, the shadows cast by the trees would appear to run parallel (as would a railroad track seen from above). If you stood on that field, the shadows cast by the trees would converge toward the horizon, whether seen from the sunny side or the shadowy side (as would our railroad track in Diagram No. 31). The shadows coming toward you would increase in size, as would a train on our tracks. The shadows going from you would decrease in size.

All my diagrams are drawn to elucidate the ordinary problems for the student. The specific and complex problems rest on these.

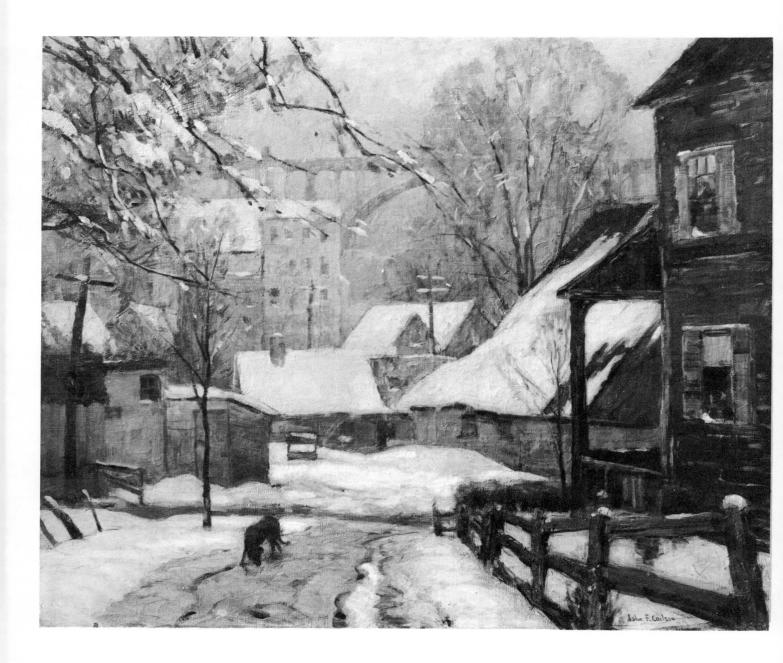

The painter, by a very slight degree of self-analysis, can select his gamuts and harmonies, as well as his constructive lines of color, rather than merely stupidly taking things as they come in nature. We must not train our eyes to copy tone for tone, but think of the bearing of such colors and harmonies upon the *main idea* of our picture.

8. COLOR

Its Emotional Value in Painting

The object of this chapter is to inquire into the psychological side of color phenomena, that is, the effect of color upon the subconscious mind of the average human being, and to ascertain what emotional reactions are produced by it. In other words, we shall consider here the artistic value of color uses.

To make our point still plainer, we will say that a picture may embody almost any color scheme so far as "color harmony" is concerned. Objects drawn upon the canvas may have almost any color for their local color. The question is, what color, or set of colors, best expresses our idea in a given picture. We must make a choice. It is quite important to inquire whether a large blue mass or a large red mass should predominate in our picture. Then there is *one* color scheme, (including the local color of any one object), one color tonality about any given canvas that more fully represents the idea of the whole picture than any other color scheme. There is even *one* local color, chosen from a myriad of possible local colors, that best represents or embodies the sense of the whole canvas—the expressiveness of it.

Study the color tonality of the canvas in which the local color is to function, and innumerable vistas of possibility will seem to open.

Color creates form. It creates the third dimension, the space around form. A color becomes beautiful when it functions as a form-creating agent. The eye and soul are caressed in the contemplation of form and color. The subtle changes of color over a surface—transitions that are like music—are intangible in their reaction upon us. There is an immediate sensuous appeal!

I know that I shall offend a great many men when I claim that aesthetic color knowledge is at all necessary in painting. By knowledge, I do not mean a "working recipe" whereby we can concoct aesthetic stimuli. I mean only that the student, by a very slight degree of self-analysis, can select his gamuts and harmonies, as well as his constructive lines, rather than merely stupidly taking things as they come in nature. We must not train our eyes to copy tone for tone, but rather our brain to think with. Think of the bearing of such ranges of color and harmonies upon the main *idea* of our picture. Only, *think with your heart!*

We will deal mainly with the aesthetic value of color combinations, or rather with the common-sense or uncommon-sense idea of the *fitness* of color combinations to the subject or idea in hand. Aside from any convention or custom, but based entirely upon the subconscious *feeling* about color, almost anyone would know better than to come attired in a bright pink dress to attend a friend's funeral. And yet, I have seen portraits of little children painted against a meaningless background of flat Cimmerian blackness (in a void, such as one might be tempted to use in painting a portrait of old Fafnir of mythology).

Whether we might call this "association of ideas" or something else, it is still true. The truth is that in choosing one color which should be analogous to youth, or life, or movement, you would not choose black, and were you to project a sensation of power, or tragedy, you would not choose pink.

Many times a painter will choose a color scheme merely because it "looks nice." There are times when a downright *ugly* scheme would be more expressive (and I do not mean as a "foil," but as an entity). "Foils," or stupid aesthetic contradictions within the same canvas, have long ago been relegated to the attic. In order that we may appreciate the enlivening rhythm of a rhumba, it is not necessary to play a dirge in the next room.

An exaggerated idea of the importance of the handling of the pigment is often the cause of artistic shortcoming. Common sense or the fitness of things is most uncommon in art. Some painters are so interested in methods of painting that even good taste is often wanting in their synthesis. They seldom analyze their feelings, but merely look. Let us dissect our feelings when we, for instance, see a bevy of children at play— the beautiful little bodies romping, brightly colored dresses speckled with sunlight. Watch them flitting across the sunlit meadow, hip-deep in daisies, their merry laughter and flowing hair all so consistent with child character. Is there anything in such a scene that would prompt anyone to snatch any of these little ones, "stick them up" and paint them against a sombre studio background of dusty blues and browns, with slate-gray hangings?

However, do not be led to believe that mere decoration or ornamentation, or mere division of spaces into agreeable proportions, filled in with any color or colors that happen to be harmonious, or that have stereotyped "transitions" into each other, is the end. In painting certain pictures it would even add artistic worth to the picture to have *disagreeable* proportions of masses, with here or there a strident color note, depending, of course, upon the character of the subject in hand.

The landscape painter is constantly har-rowed by the procession of vital changes in his light and consequent impression or effect, unless, perchance, he is merely interested in the bold facts of form and design, and not in the particular drama in which these forms and designs are actors, a drama that will never quite repeat itself in all time to come.

The very key, or general color tone enveloping the materials, mood, form and design, and the "subject" used for the creation of them, are distinguished and fine, in the measure that the artist has felt the beauty and significance of them. Let us imagine a landscape in which the forms in general have been so arranged as to produce a distinctly minor or depressing quality (this inspiration or motif for the arrangement had been impressed upon the artist by witnessing a hailstorm, let us say). Is it not true that out of a dozen different kinds of color-keys of the "ominous" blue-grey character, *one* of the keys gives a stronger feeling of ominousness than another? And when this key is added to the selection of line and mass-character in our landscape it produces a more distinct aesthetic thrill in the beholder of the picture than if we had ignored our opportunity of choice?

This is not "intellectualizing," for the emotions felt in color can never be experienced except psychologically; we are psychologically *biased* in our selection of expressive forms as well as colors. Primitive man's earliest experiences or associations play a part in the feelings we derive from different colors. One man's feelings are approximately similar to another man's, to a remarkable degree. The difference lies in *intensity* of reaction. This reaction is keener in the ordinary man than we ordinarily suspect. No man could gaze into the dark purple-blue of a storm cap and receive a joyous impression. And I do not believe that the ensuing depression of the spirit is based on fear. It may have been fear in the remote ages; it is not conscious fear now. The

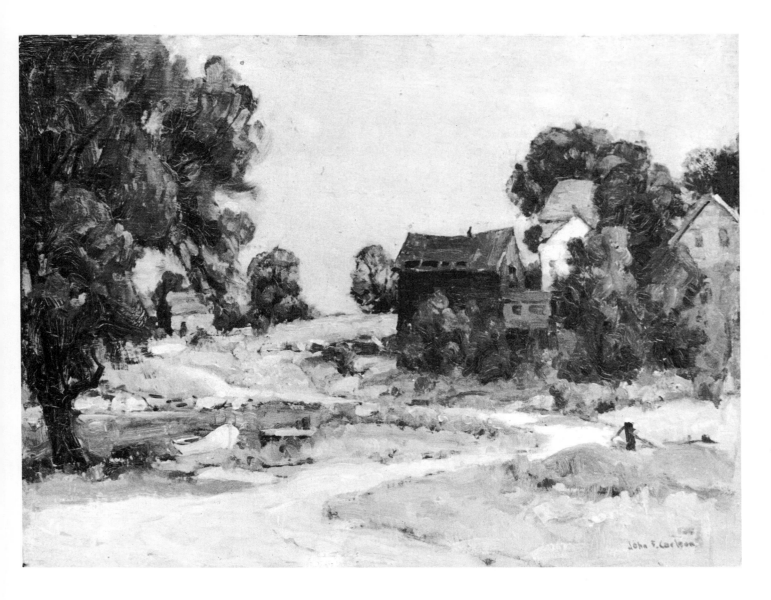

A gray day sky is lighter than a clear sky, but the diffusion of light causes a darkening of all the earth values. The very key or general color tone and "subject" of a picture must show that the artist has felt the beauty and significance of the scene.

malediction of the fading light and glooming color was probably associated with physical tragedies and retrogressions, because it caused them.

Enough for our purposes is the fact that every man reacts, and in a very similar way, to color, and to the quality and quantity of light which causes it. If a man's pride causes him to disclaim this kinship to ordinary mortals, he still feels "different" when contemplating a pearly spring morning in contrast to a stormy scene—which only proves that, after all, he's human! We are all sensitive to color-emotions, only in greater or lesser degrees. .

If you will try to conjure up before your mind's eye (or upon your palette) a series of color arrangements that will, as color *for expression's sake,* somewhat embody these abstract qualities—the tragic, the lyric, the comic—you will be helped in your understanding of the aesthetic significance of color.

"Good color" in a picture means not at all that certain prettiness that the vulgar demand. It means *expressive* color with its infinite variations, not merely color "dashed in" upon the canvas! Good color really means good taste; and "powerful" color means a reserve, to give a climax its full force, and not "red, white and blue all over."

Reserve is strength; overstatement is weakness. No one cares (as Emerson said) to hear the singer's topmost notes when the voice is "nigh on to breaking." This art of conservation is strength, and makes the masterpiece a masterpiece. Otherwise, the man who simply bought all the different colors obtainable, and squeezed them out upon the canvas to give it "full force," would be the greatest master, instead of being merely extravagant.

Color beauty is arrived at only through sensitive juxtaposition of color masses of *varying proportions,* of values and transitions. With the general growth of a student's artistic state, this color sense improves and he will eventually *feel* color rather than see it. If he is an artist he will feel when to expend and when to conserve color—the beginner's cry of "go the limit" to the contrary.

A rather easier thing to describe is the physical handling of color, that is, the "mixing," harmonizing, juxtaposing, and shading of color (pigment) and its functioning in form, and the creation of the third dimension.

To begin with, we have our triad of primary colors: red, yellow and blue. I say a "triad" constitutes the primary colors, because that theory lends itself best to our

Diagram 32: The intertwined triads of primary and secondary colors. Use of this chart helps to simplify the theory of color.

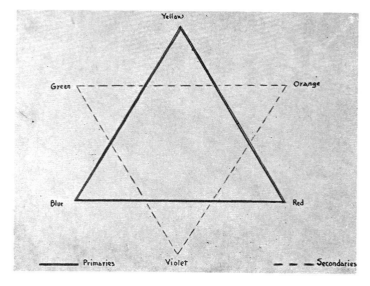

Carlson's Guide to Landscape Painting

purposes of study. According to Newton, however, the primary colors were those of the spectrum—seven in all—red, orange, yellow, green, blue, indigo, and violet. This scale comprising the principal colors and their mixture together into various hues, tints, shades, and intensities, constitutes the visional range of the human eye. (Our discussion of mixtures of color deals with the mixture of pigments, and not with colored light.) The scale of seven colors named above constitutes a large scale or gamut, from red to violet.

By "secondary colors" is meant the colors that result from a mixture of any two of the three primaries in equal proportions. (Diagram No. 32.) The secondaries are, therefore, orange (a mixture of red and yellow), violet (a mixture of red and blue), and green (a mixture of blue and yellow). The tertiary colors are those resulting from a mixture of the secondaries. The reduction of the primary, secondary or tertiary colors with white or black marks the entrance into a myriad of hues, shades, and tints. Not only does the exact color-cast of each hue, shade, and tint become more complex with each admixture, but the value scale is also more extended, ranging from deepest violet (almost black) to faintest yellow (almost white), or no color. The triad itself really comprises not only three colors, but also three values: the yellow representing the light; the red, the medium; and the blue, the dark value.

By "complementary color" is meant the rather obvious "harmony" that results from the juxtaposition of any secondary color (composed of two primaries) with the remaining primary color of the triad. Thus, if we mix yellow and red, producing an orange, the remaining blue of the triad is its complementary, etc. (all of which we have learned at school and seldom use afterwards). They constitute an easily-taught department of color study.

Color is a beautiful phenomenon; in the hands of the artist it becomes sublime, for it is made to function. The beauty of color is difficult to define. Sometimes, what is "beautiful color" to one man is not so beautiful to another. The great philosopher who can say what beauty is, abstractly, has not yet arisen. Color, when defining form, becomes lovely through the transitions it needs to undergo in receding from or approaching the eye. Even such a simple monotone thing as an egg becomes lovely in color because of this.

Color-beauty, considered from the point of color-mass harmonies, depends greatly upon *related quantities*. To illustrate this point, let us imagine that we have three color masses (poster-like) with which to decorate a given space. If that space were to be divided into three parts, the color masses would become infinitely more beautiful, were we to divide that space into three masses unequal in size. Thus, if the space given were 18 x 24 inches the division of the 24 into spaces approximately 7"-13"-4" would become more beautiful color than were the 24 divided into 8"-8"-8", assuming that we used the identical colors for our experiment. I might even assert that almost any three colors, ugly ones, would become bearable were they divided into unequal quantities. Of course, even here they would be fine, finer, finest, according to the taste (or knowledge) of the artist.

Another consideration bearing upon this same mass harmony is the value consideration of the color masses. If we were to say that a harmony made up of three masses: medium russet, medium purple, and a medium greyish-yellow (meaning medium *values* of these colors) were all in "good harmony," they would become more beautiful were they arranged in varying masses of 7"-13"-4" proportion, rather than in the masses of equal size, or 8"-8"-8". They would become still more beautiful were we to make the colors (instead of "medium" all) medium russet, dark purple, and a light grayish-yellow. In this latter harmony we have not only considered the colors as color, and their area or proportion, but we have considered their weight or value, and have added value variety to an otherwise mono-value thing. Add to the above the certain nuances or changes of shade that might be instilled into each color mass, and we have made a dynamic thing out of something that was static.

Another department entirely in the study of color is the theory of vibrational color, that is, the rendition of "light" in a picture. The theory in the main is this: It is of great advantage, especially in outdoor painting, to so apply the pigment in any given mass as to produce an *iridescent* or prismatic play of color within the mass, as against the older method of "flat" painting (painting a mass in one solid tone).

While I hold that this theory of applying pigment in no way assists inspiration or the creation of a masterpiece, yet I believe it is a thing we cannot wholly disregard—*especially* in receding tones, such as the far distance in a landscape, or the background of a portrait, is it of account. It helps in the creation of these receding tones, in the painting of these tremulous unnameable, atmospheric tones, as nothing else does. It helps us to analyze the components or different colors mixed to make a given color mass. The theory of vibratory color holds that we apply these components separately instead of mixing them together. This method of painting was discovered by the luminists, impressionists, and pointillists of the eighteen-seventies and -eighties, and it does help to give life and movement to the tones.

Much study has been expended on the subject by many worthy men. As to the question of "what color" to use in the production of any given vibratory tone, that is entirely a personal thing with each painter. The truth is that any given tone can be produced by many differing combinations

of component colors, and that the mass so produced would be identical with another in its final hue. It is a fact that the less any color is "mixed," whether on the palette or on the canvas, the clearer and more vital (even in light tones) will that color become.

For the beginner, who has trouble enough in placing his values and composing his picture, this theory of vibratory color need not be considered for some time.

One other suggestion concerning the *application* of pigment to canvas: Since there is no absolutely flat color mass in nature, we study to follow the transition or gradation that we see in the masses we are painting. In "laying in" these masses, apply the pigment generously, instead of scrubbing it in. As you proceed with the canvas, you will find color and value corrections necessary. When correcting the color of any mass, try to do it by *laying into it* the correcting tones in small touches, and without lifting the under paint up too much, or stirring it up. You will find that a certain scintillation of color accrues in such masses, that assists greatly in the feeling of "light" in the canvas For, again, no color exists (out-of-doors especially) that is not shot through with varying proportions of all the primaries, or "reductions" of the primaries.

I firmly believe that by experimenting with color—with glazing and scumbling (see Chapter 2), with different mediums and varnishes, with different ways of applying these—a knowledge of these will result that will be superior to any set formula. However, "try anything once," is good advice. Hold fast any good you get out of it, and then try something else.

It has been surprising, of late, to note the several folders and boxes issued by color manufacturers, which attempt to give the student formulas for "mixing the color" (or pre-mixed colors) of natural objects, such as trees, clouds, cows, and whatnot. To me this is an impossible thing to do, because of

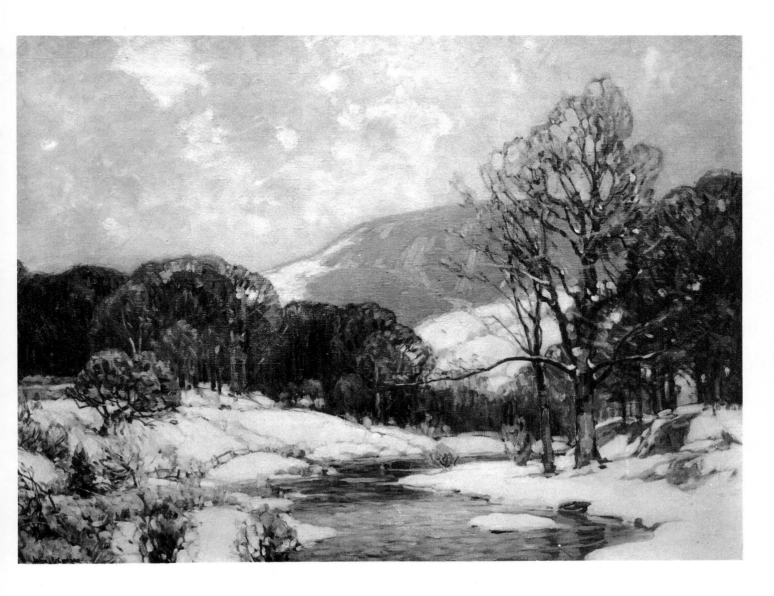

If we consider colors not only as color in an area or proportion, but also consider their weight or value, we will add value variety to an otherwise mono-value thing. Add to this the certain nuances or changes of shade that might be instilled into each color mass, and we have made a dynamic thing out of something that was static.

the *kind of light* (color or mood) in which such objects are seen (together with the so-called local color) so changes the "color" of the object, from *hour* to *hour,* that it seems not the same object at all—coloristically speaking. Besides, no two men *wish* to see color identically the same. There is a color individuality in each man. And secondly, if they did see alike, they would wish, if they were artists, to transmute what they each saw into differing expressive things. It is this fact that makes a color formula worthless, that stands in the way of all formalized color, and even interferes with the artistic creations of the formalizer.

I shall always hold that the mixing of color—its desired hue, shade or nuance—is the real thrill of painting. The sheer delight and almost surprise of abstract color variations and vibrations, and mass-harmonies! This delight is equal to that of creating line and form. Even if a sure way could be discovered for "getting the color," we could not wish to rob ourselves of the joyous uncertainty of our efforts to create color beauty!

I shall always remember how, as a student, I inquired how to mix a "cloud-gray," and received this enigmatic formula: "cobalt blue and Indian red." I was working in water color at the time and I remember spoiling many a beautiful water-color board by audacious dashes of Indian red and cobalt blue until my studio was littered. The trouble was that my informant had not stipulated any relative ratio or proportion between the two colors in question; nor did he tell me *how much water* to add to this color in order to "wash in" a pearly gray with cobalt blue and Indian red. I soon discovered that, even had it been possible for him to say: 10 per cent cobalt blue, 6 per cent Indian red and 84 per cent water, I could not, in working, have stopped to weigh out the amounts of color and water. And had I succeeded in doing so,

the result would have been a mere imitation in tone of my informant's own skies.

I have often been asked by the beginner how and why we respond to the warm or cold color gamut. Psychologically we associate actual thermal warmth with the fire colors, yellow and red. We therefore feel these as warm colors, including hues and tints partaking largely of one or both of these primaries. I have called them the "positive colors," and the "projecting colors." Likewise, and for identical reasons, we associate thermal cold with the ice colors, white and blue (and all their approximates). I have called blue, and all hues and tints partaking primarily of blue, "negative colors."

While yellow and red are "warm colors," and blue is a "cold color," there exist between these two extremes numberless half-steps or semi-warm and semi-cold colors. There are "cool yellows," which might mean a yellow that partakes considerably of white, with a modicum of blue added. There are cool and cold reds, according to the amount of white or blue added. There are warm blues—blue that partakes of red, producing a violet-blue, or a blue that partakes of both red and white, which produces a colder, lighter violet-blue. Again, the blue might partake of a modicum of yellow which produces a greenish-blue, or blue with yellow and white added, which produces a colder, lighter blue, or greenish-blue.

All reductions of pure blue with yellow or red are warm blues. Naturally, if we sway this blue still farther toward the yellow, or toward the red, we arrive at last at green, on the yellow side, and violet on the red side, both of which are warm secondaries. All the colors named can be reduced or "grayed" by the addition of black or white, or by adding certain portions of their complementaries.

The resulting myriads of half-steps, or semi-tones in the mixing of colors no man

Carlson's Guide to Landscape Painting

can define to the entire satisfaction of individual color perception in different individuals. And even *if* abstract names could be fastened to the multitude of hues, shades and tints, what good would it do the artist? Such pigeon-holing of a faculty is harmful, and can be useful only to the manufacturer.

In fussing with and mixing these tones, hues and shades, you will sometimes discover, "by accident," this or that color (very much as when you are struggling with the lines and areas of a composition, and some accident helps you solve the problem). Yet these things are not truly accidental. What seems to be pure chance is really the accumulated force of many previous efforts or *lesser results*. Nothing can come out of nothing; this is especially true in art. It requires intelligence to take advantage of the "accident." Do not, therefore, be ashamed of it. You supplied the impulse, and are now only required to steer it. Without the impulse, steering would be impossible; without the steering, impulse would lack direction.

As interesting reading, the study of color (as light) from the scientific point of view, its physical make-up, etc., will do no harm. Color is defined in Webster's as "a quality of visible phenomena, distinct from form and from light and shade." It depends upon the light of different wave-lengths on the retina of the eye. But the student of painting can do without the detailed scientific data. It is enough that a painter sees color, and is moved by it, and can apply its aesthetic uses to his needs.

Successful use of color in painting will come with study. Ultimately, a picture should really be so well synthesized or organized in color that, were it turned upside down (the subject matter thereby becoming unrecognizable), the color relations and transitions would in themselves (as abstract color) express the idea of the picture. This is an extreme statement to make to beginners, who must first master simpler concepts; I mention it here as an ideal for final attainment.

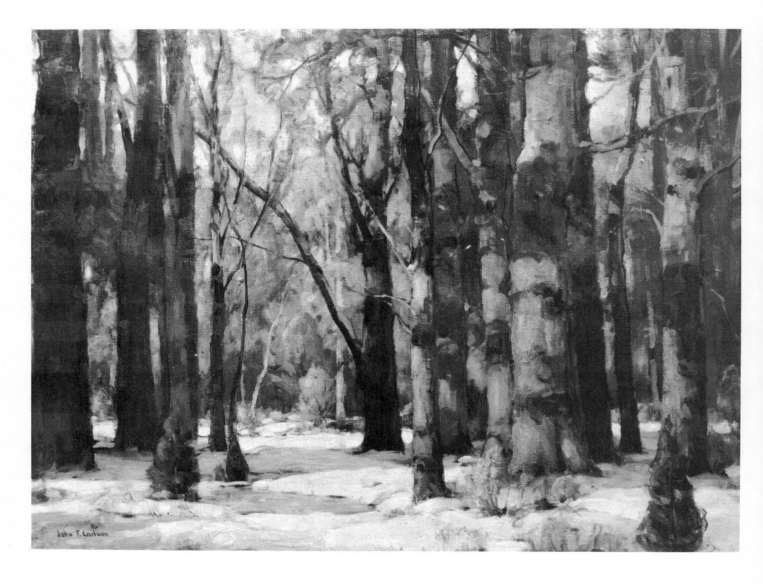

You will learn to paint trees only by understanding them, their growth, their nature, their movement—and realizing that they are conscious living things. A tree seldom if ever encroaches upon the liberty of another tree. It never wastes its growth in unnecessary twistings. To the artist, the forest is an asylum of peace and dancing shadows.

9. TREES

How to Understand Them

"How do you paint a tree?" The beginner always imagines that by some trick of the wrist, some mysterious sleight of hand—by some special manner of "putting on" paint —a tree can be painted.

When the answer comes, "By understanding trees," it may seem more or less enigmatic. Yet this is the answer. As in any art, so in painting, the necessary knowledge takes almost a lifetime to acquire and cannot be handed on a silver platter to one who has made no effort to gain it.

It is easy enough to gain sufficient technical knowledge in six weeks to "put on paint," but you may spend a lifetime studying trees without knowing all about them. You may paint your tree any way you wish, and the less your method looks like some other man's, the happier you should be. Paint your tree any way you wish, but get the tree.

Know your trees, their nature, their growth, their movement; understand that they are conscious, living things, with tribulations and desires not wholly disassociated from your own. Emerson has beautifully named trees, "rooted men." In many ways they excel man.

A tree seldom or never encroaches upon the liberty of another tree, if it can be avoided. Usually "both parties" settle equitably, and without "due process." A tree recognizes that its liberty ends where the next tree's liberty begins. A tree never wastes its growth in unnecessary twistings, nor in frivolous waste of energy. If a tree is seen to twist and turn (within its type's specific scope), these turns and twists are intimately connected with, or in rapport with, the turnings and twistings of a neighboring tree. This engenders a certain rhythm or flow of related lines in a wood.

To the insensitive or unfeeling, a wood merely represents a heterogeneous multitude of vertical sticks. A good "stand of trees" means dollars and cents: or perhaps a place where one can hunt. To the artist the forest is an asylum of peace, of dancing shadows, of sun-flecked green. The rugged trunks are stalwart guardians—green, violet, and russety grey—with their reaching branches meeting in a noble arch overhead. An eloquent silence, made up of a myriad of pleasant sounds, seems to hang in the air. Hundreds of little eyes gleam timidly from their refuges; small ears are alert to determine the intention of an intruder. (If the snow is upon the ground, you may see footprints upon its soft surface.)

Every tree is a "personality," and possesses, within the limits of its species, a tremendous latitude of expression. Its branches do not, could not, and should not, stick into its sides in a brittle way, as though a hole had previously been bored to let them in. A tree is a highly organized entity, which, when functioning in its realm, becomes beautiful. There is a limit to its functions, and if you *realize* this, you will never, for "artistic reasons," so deform a tree as to make it ridiculous. If you do not understand this, then nothing can hinder you from painting a tree on its head, roots in air, for "artistic reasons."

A tree is a very useful piece of material in landscape painting, and can be moved about in your composition. Treat it in your composition as you would a heroic man. Do not approach trees with that flip, blasé superiority that has always stood in the way of serious appreciation in this world. Do not think that a tree can be translated into paint by slapstick and trowel technique. Instead, go buy a good pad of drawing paper, and on each page draw a tree. One such study, of one such tree, will teach you at the start how much you need to know.

It is curious how one's feelings about trees change, in proportion to one's appreciation of their importance and dignity as *live beings*. Trees are *individual* beings: they can be comic, heroic, tragic to the sensitive, practiced eye of the landscape artist.

The painting of trees is best accomplished by much drawing of trees. When we are *painting* we get excited by so many things that it is hard to stoop to imitative drawing. In spare hours, when we are not painting, we can apply ourselves with pencil and pad, getting the likeness or main character of trees. You will find that this drawing is not a drudgery; it is only another way of expressing the tree. Do not be afraid to make these drawings "literal" for some time to come. When you go back to the swing of painting, you will find that your literal knowledge will stand you in good stead. You almost have to learn to *make* a thing, before you can paint it with understanding.

Study what the different trees *do,* as well as how one species differs in the main from another. Try to find out what the principal differentiation in character is between, say, an apple tree and a sycamore. Not that you are going to incorporate this knowledge into a treatise on this difference but, having *noted* the difference in character, you will see many other new qualities in these specimens, and in many other things besides. Your powers of analysis will be that much strengthened. An intelligent synthesis, a kind of insight into the fitness of things, will result. This will finally develop into a feeling for the significant qualities abiding in objective nature. It is this last that differentiates the artist from the student.

Consider our apple trees! All apple trees are alike, as a species, and yet—see the great difference between one apple tree and another! It is wonderful to see that whatever the compound and complex movement of any tree's branches, its "growth," its rhythmic reaching out and pulling back, its swirl and gnarl, or its seeming static indifference, all are in perfect accord with the "type." All are in "character."

The specific life-germ that established the differing species in differing climes is as mysterious today as ever. We have, as Carlyle says, proceeded but a hand's-breadth into the mysteries of nature. It is enough that we have the apple tree, that it is beautiful and that it gives fruit; that we have the oak, and that it yields acorns and a grateful shade. In the apple seed and in the acorn live all future apple trees and oaks. The same moisture seeping through the same earth, when absorbed by the roots of the oak, produces acorns; when by the apple tree, apples.

"It will take study and time," is the only answer to the question as to how to paint a tree, or anything else, for that matter.

Trees are elusive! Nature sometimes seems to have especially created them to tease beginners in landscape painting. With sympathetic understanding, we are apt to feel a tree more keenly. Trees are the most personal objects in a landscape; we feel distinctly related to them. The vast sky or the gloomy mountain are far removed from us —they are like a distant, deep organ note. They are dictators of conditions; they even influence the weather. The trees, like ourselves, are the humble recipients.

When compared with trees, foreground elements such as weeds, or flowers, or shrubs are not imposing personalities, are but mere children that we banter with or caress. Anyone who has walked through a forest, espe-

Carlson's Guide to Landscape Painting

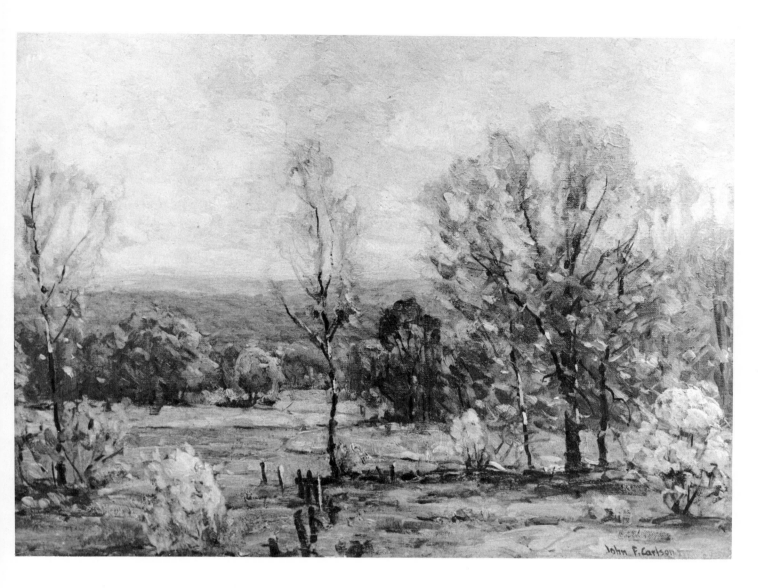

Taper is not only in the main spine or trunk, but in every limb starting from it. The trunk visibly begins at the ground, with a bulk commensurate with the tree's height and the weight of its foliage.

cially in winter, will not wonder at these imputations of personality to trees. They stand there, silent and dignified, but never unfriendly. We almost feel that they would speak in a rich, low voice, were we to address them. Closer study of their habits and doings (for both words are applicable) will only enhance this feeling of personality in trees, and increase our aesthetic delight in their form and color.

Earlier we alluded to trees as mere upright planes or masses supported by a stem or trunk. We saw in the chapter on linear perspective how trees as a mass grew a trifle lighter and cooler as they ascended into the light of the sky—always bearing in mind the lateral or side-gradation determined by the position of the direct light falling upon the mass from any quarter of the sky. We come now to the problem of constructing or drawing these masses we have called trees.

Let us say that we have proceeded with our tree thus far: after determining the place that the tree or trees are to occupy in our picture, and the size of the mass we wish to create, we have roughly drawn the main outline or general contour upon the canvas with a brush dipped in some medium dark tone or shade upon the palette, after which we have filled in this mass with approximate general local color and value, grading it from top to bottom, and from side to side, to meet the requirements already stated. (Diagram No. 4.) We have thus far neglected the drawing of branches, of traceries, and sky-holes (except a few of the largest ones) through the tree. We merely have a simple, semi-flat mass of the approximate color, conforming somewhat to the outline shape of the tree we are painting, and possessing as nearly as possible the exact degree of value or darkness in relation to ground and sky.

Certain vital elements in this makeup must now be considered, such as growth, movement, and character. We begin by noting that all trees have one quality in com-

mon: they possess a spine, or trunk, visibly beginning at the base or ground, with a bulk commensurate with their height and the weight of their foliage. This spine gradually tapers upward to the highest crown and, of course, also descends into the ground. There, with numerous lateral multiforms of the same spine, called roots, the tree maintains its base in the earth.

These roots often extend for greater distances than the branches of the tree. Some trees also have what is called a taproot that descends vertically deep into the ground, forming a kind of anchor. And all these roots are eminently needed to support the tree in a vertical plane, because of the tremendous force the wind exerts in its attacks upon the foliage. It is this need of great strength that causes a tree seemingly to grasp the earth as with a giant claw, and it is this need of strength that causes the spine to taper continuously to the top crown.

The average tree trunk, compared with the mass of the tree's leaves or branches above the first low branch, is usually no larger than the stem of an apple, compared with the apple.

After having drawn the main shape and the correct proportions of your tree, study the deviations of the branches from the main trunk. Note how the smaller branches leave the larger ones, how the still smaller branches leave the smaller ones, and finally how the twigs at the extreme end of every branch leave these. This constant and *gradual* diminution of thickness, from trunk to tendril, is the most important factor in painting a tree so that it will look like a growing thing. This constant taper gives size, flow, and dignity to your tree. Neglect it, and your tree is "nice color" or some other inane thing. Every tree has a distinct apex, or high point, and it is toward this apex that your main trunk meanders or reaches. (Diagram No. 33.)

The constant tapering, the deviations and meanderings of trunk and branches are a

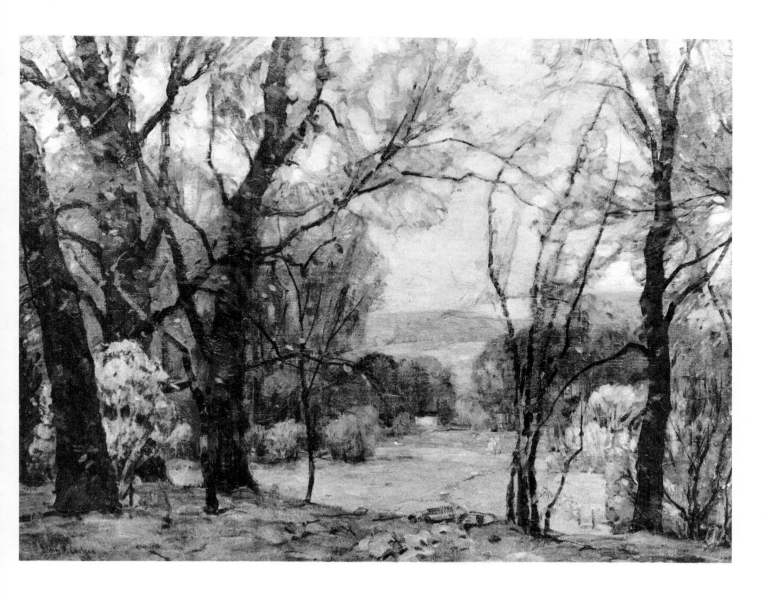

The constant and gradual diminution of thickness in the trunk and branches of a tree, in the limbs and twigs, right out to the smallest point, is the most important factor in painting a tree so that it will look like a living, growing thing.

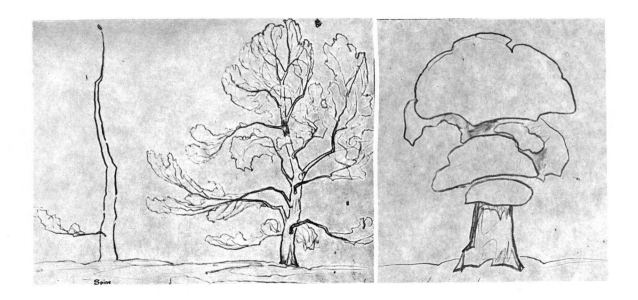

Spine

Diagram 33: It is towards the apex that the main trunk tapers and reaches.

Diagram 34: This mushroom-like tree will never taper fast enough to come to a point at its apex.

little different in each species of tree. Elements of environment probably decide the degree of difference in each tree, its individual character.

The beginners who try to make their trees "big" by filling the whole canvas with their tree, from top to bottom, should remember that a very big thing cannot be seen at all if you get too close to it! If you fill your canvas with a tree, the very fact that it "stands on the frame" makes it feel like a near object, and its reaction on the subconscious mind is: "If it is so near, and still can be seen in entirety, it is not very big." (Diagram No. 35.)

If you want "big trees," and want them right near the foreground, show only a *small portion* of them, and they will look big. (Diagram No. 43.) Or else set them back from the foreground as in Diagram No. 27.

A fast-growing tree is always distinguishable by its straighter spine. In the slow-growing tree we find the spine performing greater or lesser contortions, varying in degree according to the age of the trees. In the hurried shoot of the rapidly-growing

type, we recognize a gentle tangential, as against the suddenly hooked gnarl of the slow-growing type; also a more horizontal extension in the main branches. Thus we have a "gnarled oak," and a "graceful flowing birch." It is almost as if the oak, like some athlete, slowly develops its large and strong muscles in order to support the tre-

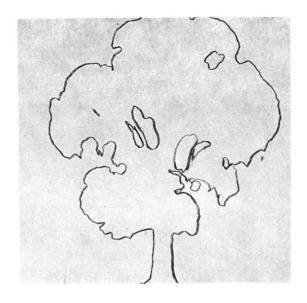

Diagram 35: A big tree cannot be seen at all if placed too near in the foreground.

mendous "clouds" of foliage. No one wonders at this who has tried to hold a fully-leaved oak bough (even a very small one) at arm's length! The leverage is tremendous at the base or union of any large branch with the trunk. An oak will hold horizontally a branch measuring as much as twenty-five feet. It would require a dozen men to perform the same feat. It is no wonder, therefore, that the union of such a branch to the main trunk is effected with much ramification. The branch suddenly widens at the base (or where it joins the main trunk), and is moulded or flanged into the trunk so as to withstand the strain which it is expected to bear. This ramification does not cease at the surface of the trunk, but rather continues into the tree, almost to the heart of it. We appreciate this when we see a trunk sawed into boards; the knots and surrounding circular markings represent the "roots" of branches.

Assuming now that we have established upon our canvas a tree of sufficient excellence of form and gradations *to look like a tree,* it then behooves us to begin a building-up of its smaller forms within the larger: to separate the groups of foliage which make up its main bulk; to draw the visible trunks and branches; to study the character of the edges (where the tree's *texture* is most easily seen), and finally to add such detail of highlight and accent as are needed.

I have relegated the so-called "detail drawing" to a minor place in our progress. This drawing is the least important and easiest to do in the painting of trees. The most important part of the drawing is the establishment of functioning masses. Adding the frills merely requires time.

When the trunks and branches are only intermittently visible, as in a tree with heavy foliage, it is difficult to follow the degree of taper of each. Extreme care is recommended in the painting of these. (Diagram No. 27.) Begin by gently building up the light places, or lighted parts of the tree, and introducing

darker darks into the shadowy places of your tree. The general mass that was primarily established before such modelling took place represents the "medium-dark value"—that is, neither the lighted portions nor the darkest portions of the tree. The temptation in adding lights to a tree is to add *too much light,* so that the mass becomes cut up and loses its proper value-relation. Study the color transitions or gradations while modelling this mass. The soundness or solidity of the tree rests mostly upon the just value-relation to other planes, but the beauty and atmosphere rest upon the sensitive color transitions.

In nature, trees differ in color tremendously. Add to this the color of the light thrown upon it and it is obvious that the color must be left to the individual observer and the specific light effect.

The main admonition here is: place the tree-as-a-mass in true value-relation with the other mass-elements, such as the sky and ground, and it will be comparatively easy to determine all the color phenomena above noted, with all their changes and subtleties. Trust your *feelings* entirely about color, and then, even if you arrive at no infallible color theory, you will at least have the credit of having your own color sense.

Remember that the most realistic landscape in the world *can* be a work of art, but do not think that because a landscape is "real" that it is a work of art. A true picture is one in which so-called natural elements are made to function as an idea.

Let us imagine that we are painting a hickory tree, whose background is composed of sky and distant hills. Invariably, the novice will paint the sky-holes or interstices between the foliage groups *too light.* It is a fact that none except possibly the largest sky-holes in a tree are as light as the sky. If you paint them as light as you think they are, they will invariably look as though some light spots had been pasted upon your tree. They stick out and refuse to allow the eye to go through the tree. The quantity of light allowed to come through any sky-hole naturally varies with the size of the hole. This establishes the fact that the smaller the hole the darker is the sky looking through it.

Diffraction accounts for the "atmospheric edge," together with the fact that light diffuses itself over the edges of any dark object placed against it, lightening that mass very slightly. Obviously enough, the darkening of the light mass shown through a dark surrounding is not confined to holes through the trees, but to that portion of the sky or light mass that visibly intrudes itself between the festoons of foliage at the undulating *outline of the tree* against the sky. This "losing" of the light at the edges is not affected by diffraction as much as are the interstices of sky completely surrounded by dark (such as the holes *through* a tree). This law is applicable to light-and-dark masses of every variety.

All lights as they go back lose some of their brilliance. Much care must be taken, however, that these differences be infinitesimal, but the ignoring of them entirely is as fatal as any overdoing. So much for this study of light.

Although trees are the most important objects in our out-of-door nature, bushes and shrubs may be considered as part and parcel of the upright plane. They are of dark value, excepting, of course, shrubs in bloom or flowering bushes, whose local color is lighter than the plain shrub. The character of the shrub or bush, however, is quite different from that of trees, even young trees. The fork-like branchings of the bush begin very near the ground (in some cases under it, resulting in "shoots"). The bush usually has several stems of almost equal importance, some of their number drying up as the bush grows treeward, finally allowing only the strongest one to survive. Do not draw bushes that look like trees in miniature. (Diagram No. 37.)

The greatest deviation from the straight line in the spine of a tree usually occurs at the juncture of an important branch. The branch, in gaining importance, forces the parent spine or trunk away from itself by an instinct in the tree to balance itself over its center of gravity. (Diagram No. 37.) The next branch above, and on the opposite side, forces it back again toward the vertical.

I have seen a fine "compound" example of this action in the case of a young birch planted too near a rain gutter of my house. The tree grew straight and beautiful until its apex touched the rain trough, then it stopped. There gradually became noticeable a curious thickening of one of the branches near the top of the tree, and farthest away from the house. As the branch thickened, the main branch which had "stopped" seemed to shrivel, with the result that the first branch gradually semi-circled and cleared the trough by almost a foot, and then began to go straight up again, continuing the line that the main spine had originally intended to follow. The former main spine gradually, and modestly, became a mere branch above the point of junction. A severe departure from the straight line of any trunk at its juncture with the branches is never a mere "whim" of the tree.

All trunks and branches taper, except the viny growths. These are sometimes thicker at varying distances from the root than the root itself. I have said previously that the branches of a tree usually begin about ten feet from the ground. This refers to isolated trees. In a dense forest the lower branches drop away as superfluous in the race for the light of the sky. Besides, a tree is not prone to shoot, or extend a branch laterally, where the forest is dense. Remember that each tree has a wholesome respect for its neighbor. The trees in a forest are therefore tall, straight, and tapering, with foliation taking place near the top.

After giving precedence to the main spine, every tree has very marked important branches or limbs. Its other branches are,

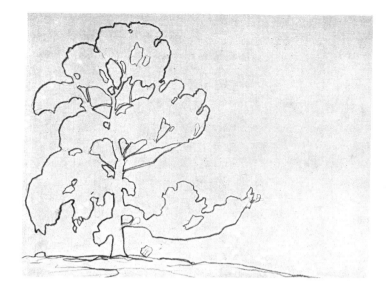

Diagram 36: Five or six understood sky-holes can establish a tree, minus all detail.

for the most part, mere offshoots of the main branches or main trunk. These main branches divide our tree into a few simple masses or colonies of foliage. To grasp the significance of these large masses as colonies of foliage belonging to a tree, will enable us to dispense with a whole lot of useless "leaf-painting." (We may paint leaves forever, and yet not paint a tree.) As we recognize how the foliage masses are attached to these main branches, and the branches to the tree, how the lesser branches belong to one or another of the larger limbs, our tree becomes "simple." It becomes more decorative for the same reason.

The final painting of our beloved highlights, as well as of the smaller "branchage," should be only as embellishments upon our large foliage masses or colonies of foliage. Our tree has thus become, instead of a rack bearing myriads of unattached leaves, a simple, constructive, growing form, with a few simple forms within it. The ability to "colonize" the masses of a tree before paying any attention to its leaves is the first step toward making the tree not only structural but decorative. It is, in fact, "how to paint a tree."

The most important sky-holes, coming between the big colonies of foliage (rather

Diagram 37: The character of bushes is quite different from that of trees, even young trees. A bush begins to branch out very near the ground. In a tree, the greatest deviation from the vertical line usually occurs at the juncture of an important branch.

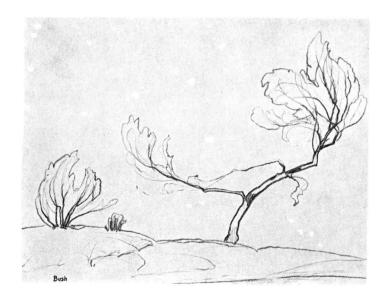

Bush

than "any old place"), now begin to mean something. Diagram No. 36 shows how five or six understood sky-holes can establish a tree, minus all detail. One can feel where the main branches must come, even when they cannot be seen for the foliage. This colonization of foliage masses is best understood after we have drawn numberless bare trees (without foliage), for then we see, obviously enough, that bare branches are arranged by nature into large groups of branches within the tree, rather than into a harum-scarum network. A tree reaches for the light with its every leaf, and therefore nature has made a tree into large groups of foliage, to allow a greater surface of the tree to be exposed to light.

When you paint those decorative holes, which either make or break the tree, it is well to note the colonization of the tracery masses so that your holes may *function,* and not be mere spots. Again, all the masses of tracery that the tree possesses can be traced as belonging to one or another important (primary or secondary) branch.

Every tree, therefore, besides having three or four or five important *carrying branches,* also has, of necessity, four or five important "sky-holes," or dividing spaces. When this quality of a tree is understood, any amount of detail, even finical drawing, may be added without impairing the decorative simplicity of the tree. Of course, as was said of the branches and twigs, there are primary, secondary, and tertiary sky-holes that must be painted into the tree, but these sky-holes have their own place in the rendition of tracery, and they never intrude themselves upon the notice at the expense of the large structural holes.

When thus seen, the numberless small sky-holes that permeate a colony of small twigs are so reduced in intensity (through being small), and the small twigs themselves are so reduced in darkness, that together they become a mere scumbly, fuzzy "cloud" of a half-value, but with a *distinct* edge or boundary. Try to master this idea, and bare trees will lose half their terror for you. To observe the above, look with half-closed eyes at some "lacy" tree.

One more word: In the painting or drawing of trees, try to make something that is more than a mere fan-like shape in two dimensions with branches running through it—something that has bulk to it. Even the laciest of trees spreads out in all directions, and is therefore of some depth. You will find, as a general help, that all the branches that come toward you are darker than those going away from you: the former present their underside to view (shadow), while the latter present their top (lighted) planes.

After making a great number of "tight" drawings of trees, try to preserve what you have gained, and then try to make your subsequent drawings more expressive of some abstract movement of your tree. You will find that some trees appear to dance, others to reach, others to curtsy, others to sulk, others to stand at attention. In searching for these "gestures" of your trees, you are preparing yourself for artistic *uses* of your trees. Do not, however, let this use destroy one iota of beauty in your tree. Let your tree be doing something, but do not let that something "do" the tree. The more we advance, the more we realize with Whistler that nature is never right. We change things, and move things, and eliminate things, all for the artistic needs of line and mass, color and expression.

If you want a "certain line," do not use a tree to do the work unless the tree itself conforms. Do not *lie* about a tree, but use some other object to give the line. A work of art seldom or never features a physical lie. The disease of trying-to-be-different is a bad malady. No great artist stoops to charlatanism to arrive at results.

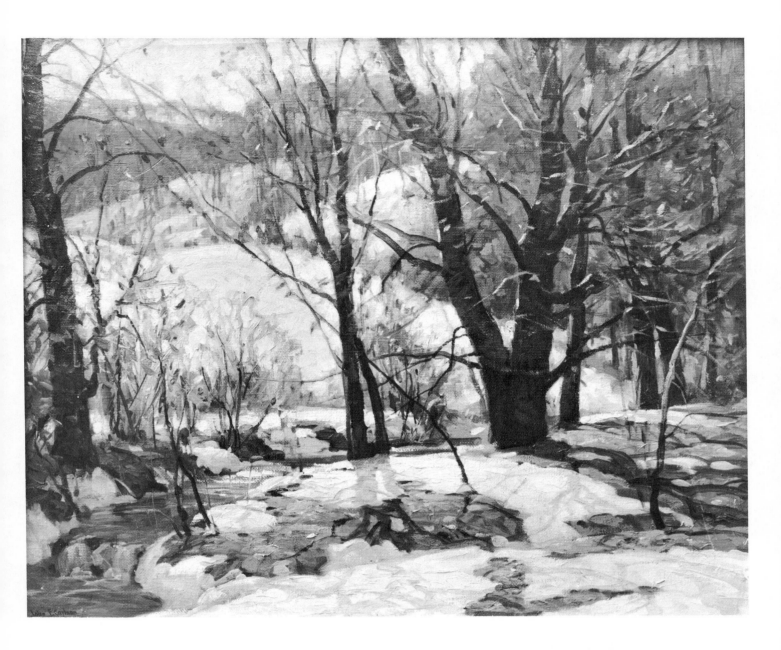

Trees branch in all directions. Try to draw a tree that is more than a mere fan-like shape in two dimensions with branches running through it—something that has bulk to it. Even the laciest of trees spreads out in all directions, and is therefore of some depth. You will find that all the branches that come toward you are darker than those going away from you, and that the former present their underside to view, while the latter present their top planes to view.

10. CLOUDS

How They Float

While a treatise upon the physical constituents and the meteorological significance of clouds might be thought of no importance to the landscape painter, I have always in my own work felt a need for it. Whatever technical knowledge I acquired about clouds did not, in any way, detract from my appreciation of their beauty, nor from their use for my needs. On the contrary, it gave the clouds a personality and individuality of their own. They no longer were mere white-on-blue paint (for the painter sees everything in paint), but became "agents" of dynamic forces. No longer were they merely arranging themselves in beautiful orderly disorder to please my vision, but each cloud became an individual, performing duties that were closely bound up with my own physical existence. Without penetrating very deeply into the science of nephology, I found myself gaining an increasing respect for clouds. They assumed a dignity which in no way lessened the glory of the sky.

The sky is the key to the landscape. Its majesty permeates outdoor nature. It is the dictator of conditions and of moods—not alone the moods of nature, but our own as well. I know that there are men who never see the sky at all. A certain plain man of our hills at Woodstock once said: "You know, before you artists got here, I never used to see the sky."

I think the sky stimulates the imagination and our aesthetic sensibility more than any other out-of-door element. If we do not feel it when painting, it is lost. In relation to a prevailing outdoor mood or effect, a certain consistency of character is the prime quality of the sky—it makes the mood. This consistency reaches into the design of each separate cloud, and is repeated in the whole, on a larger scale. There is a consistency of color relation, since the colors are visibly steeped in the quality of the prevailing light. All are born of the sky.

If you do not believe that this consistency is a necessary factor in a picture, try to paint a dark, gloomy, turbulent and windswept landscape, with hulking, pushing forms (like evil spirits) scudding across the vision, and then paint above this landscape a serene, smiling pale-blue sky with stratus clouds floating lazily along. Your picture will not only be ridiculous in its psychological and physical ambiguities, but ugly in its color relations as well.

I have pictured the above for your imagination to bring home to you the idea that even a slight knowledge of natural phenomena will increase your appreciation of beauty. It will occasionally assist you in making choices of importance when working from imagination. If nothing more, a certain knowledge prevents us from perpetrating blunders that might seem ridiculous in a thing devoted to artistic dignity.

It will not hurt you to know that some clouds float in a depressing nearness to the earth, and even drag on it (as in the case of a fog), nor that some clouds float in the rarefied atmosphere of tremendous height. The very knowledge that the sky is a great fluid-floating void may help you to paint a sky that is more than a pattern, or mere gradation of color.

Clouds are fascinating to paint (just for

their own sake) because they are the only element in landscape painting that possesses free movement. Because they change their place so steadily, the beginner needs to know something about them before attempting to paint them. In the same way a portrait painter will study a child he is going to paint—knowing that the child will never really "pose" for him.

Physics makes it plain that a cloud is a visible assemblage of minute particles of water or ice, condensed into visibility or denser bulk by the cooler temperatures of great heights. These vapors hang suspended (as clouds) at various heights, and the altitudes somewhat determine their form or character. Condensation results from cooling. Hot vapor is invisible. The hot vapor (or steam) inside the cylinder of a steam engine is compressed invisible vapor, until its expansion and final expulsion takes place. It bursts forth from the exhaust in a white cloud and disappears—parts of it condensing into drops of water, and particles of it being absorbed and evaporated into the air.

A cloud is like such steam vapor that has risen from the warmer earth, and, rising into cooler air strata, suddenly becomes visible.

A curious and unconscious idea about clouds is prevalent among us all, that clouds *come* from some quarter and *go* to some other quarter. This is true only part of the time. At times clouds form and float away from right above our heads. At other times clouds come from "somewhere," dissolve and disintegrate, and disappear as they come into our neighborhood.

For this reason, a sky that is clear may within minutes become completely overcast, or vice versa. The invisible vapors, present at all times, rise or are swept upward by an air current, and suddenly form into clouds. The clouds may as suddenly be gone.

Of course, the feeling that the clouds are always "coming" from somewhere is the artistic one. Clouds are always on the move,

fast or slow; this movement may, for its gesture, be very important to the artist. Movement is the most important thing. The mere arranging of the clouds into a pattern or design may otherwise be a dead ornamentation.

In the scientific categories there are four principal varieties of clouds, formed according to the altitude and quality of the air currents: cumulus, stratus, cirrus, and nimbus, with their half-steps between, formed from more or less conflicting conditions.

The cumulus is usually present (in its truest form) in the quiet hot air of a late afternoon and is especially native to the eastern sky, or opposite the nearly-setting sun. Cumulus clouds also appear at other times and places besides, and differ greatly. A wind-blown cumulus, for instance, becomes similar to some big, fuzzy-furry animal, hulking along. This is not strange when we consider the ocean-like character of the upper air. There are true waves, eddies, whirlpools, pockets, maelstroms, rivers, and wild-rushing torrents to be found there. Sometimes these run at confused cross-purposes, as in the hurricane. All seem independent in speed or direction from the air strata next to them. Each stratum has its own independent temperature. (Of course, we know that it is the great differences in temperatures and air densities that create the upheavals of the air.)

Turner, at his best, was a master at the building of a sky. Wyant, too, with his oft-repeated combination of cumulus relieved against stratus, understood his skies. I recommend this understanding of clouds to the beginner, and suggest that he make repeated and "tight" studies of the many skies that attract him. Even if these studies are mere maps, he will learn, while doing them, much that will be useful in his future pictures. The sky is the key to the landscape, because of the *quality* and *quantity* of the light falling from it. It determines color unity and value contrast of the remaining elements; it even determines the exact force of their forms within a given unity.

The cumulus clouds range in altitude above the earth from 5,000 feet to 15,000 feet; the stratus, or "sheet clouds" range from 2,000 to 7,000 feet. The cirrus, or "mare's-tail clouds" usually occur at 20,000 to 40,000 feet, and are mostly composed of fine ice-crystals. The nimbus, or rain-clouds, are the low-hanging, water-soaked clouds, obscuring the light, and at times dragging on the lower hills. Because of their diverse density and altitude all these clouds differ greatly in color and value. All of them, because of the arching back of the sky, also grade in color with a speed determined by the conditions of the atmosphere. The atmosphere consists of small particles of vapor suspended in the component gases of the air. Into this both land and sky recede (from foreground to horizon, and from zenith to horizon). It has the ambiguous quality of *cooling* (in color) and lightening all darks (slightly) and darkening or dulling (slightly) all the whites or near-whites, as they recede from the eye. (For further discussion of the atmosphere, see the chapter on Aerial Perspective.)

The ordinary white cumulus and stratus clouds of the summer day recede in color as follows: the whites and near-whites of the clouds go back a trifle warmer and darker towards the horizon, while the cloud "bases" or actual shadow portions of clouds go back a trifle cooler and lighter towards the horizon. The "blue" of a blue sky, which comes under the head of light (and is probably "lighter than you think"), goes back from a resonant blue at the zenith, slightly lightening and *warming* (with a modicum of green) toward the still lighter and greener zone (a modicum of yellow added), until it gradually assumes a milky, pale, yellowish green; descending then to a smokier and slightly darker warm gray-violet hue (a modicum of red added), until the horizon is reached.

Upon this graded surface of the blue sky, let us observe the cumulus clouds. These are whitest in color and lightest in value near the overhead (or zenith). As they recede into the middle sky a slight warming of the whites can be observed, which increases as the distance increases, slightly warming and slightly darkening or dulling these whites—until they approach the horizon. Here they actually assume a rosy, warm white of dull value. In other words, the whites seem to follow the warming of the blue against which they appear. Look suddenly from these rosy-white clouds at the horizon to the white clouds at the zenith, and you will be surprised at the obviousness of the gradation.

The "base" of a cloud refers almost entirely to the cumulus and nimbus types. Obviously enough, the heavier and bulkier the cloud, the more pronounced its base. A cumulus cloud somewhat resembles a soap-bubble floating upon the water, its top rounded, its bottom flat. These clouds rest at a given air level at varying altitudes, governed by the relative density and temperature of both air and cloud. These bases come under the head of "darks," and as all darks become lighter and cooler in color as they recede, so do these bases of clouds. The color and value changes in such bases must necessarily be *slight,* however, since they occur upon the lightest (in color) element or mass in our landscape.

By carefully studying the relative values of clouds and earth, the "float" of the cloud is made more natural. Do not get the idea that dark clouds are darker than your earth values. These dark clouds obstruct the light that would otherwise fall upon the earth, causing the *earth* value to become darker than usual. All beginners (in their anxiety to get the clouds dark enough) forget this truth, and for that reason their clouds often become so heavy that they never could be suspended in mid-air.

Let me say here that the lateral or side

Carlson's Guide to Landscape Painting

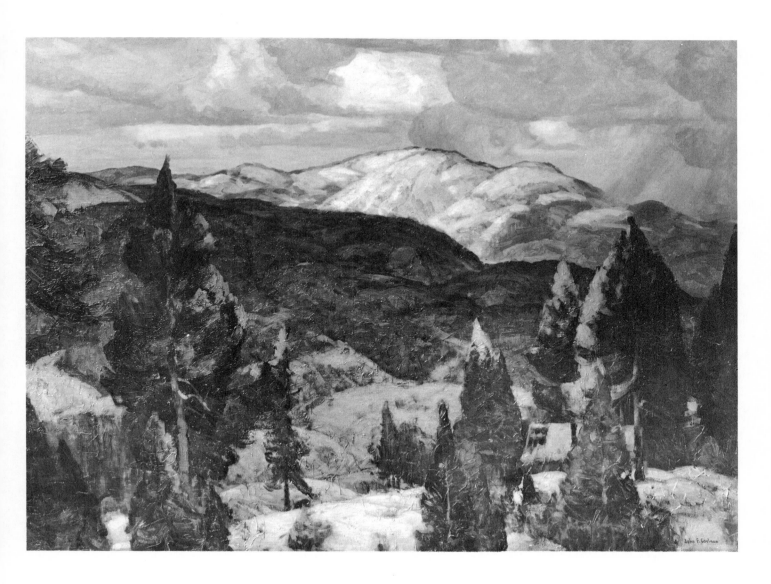

Clouds are fascinating to paint because they are the only element in a landscape that possesses free movement. Clouds are always on the move, fast or slow. Movement is the most important thing. The mere arranging of clouds into a pattern or design may otherwise be a dead ornamentation. Let the clouds float. They will be stronger and more beautiful if they seem to be functioning as clouds in the air, than if you make them half-rocks.

gradations mentioned in aerial perspective apply, of course, to clouds as well as to the blue of the sky. We have dealt mostly with vertical gradations of color from zenith to horizon. Once we establish this firmly, it will be easy to note the lateral gradations. There are but slight color changes in these side gradations, only a slight difference in the value, as they recede from the light. Obviously, if the source of light is of warm hue there will be a cooling of tones as they leave this source, and vice versa.

Probably the most difficult and baffling thing about the painting of clouds is the rendering of their edges. Invariably the beginner will attempt a cloud by loading the canvas with daubs of white paint, and when his clouds "won't model," he is much discouraged.

In the first place, clouds are very rarely pure white, especially as they recede. Besides, they have form within their puzzling flatness. Their "near-whiteness" is, therefore, not completely flat but modelled with the bulbous form of the cloud. Since the cloud is a modeled or rounded mass, the whitest or lightest tones are never near the *edge,* except when the cloud is interposed between you and the sun, when it shows its "silver lining." Daubing on of too much pigment (actually making a texture where but little texture should be) and the erroneous conception that the highest light is at the edges of clouds, often cause the painted clouds of beginners to look as though they were pasted *on* the blue sky, rather than floating *in* it.

"I want to make a strong sky," says one student. In that case put the "strength" in rocks and trees and mountains, and let the clouds *float* and be strong. Clouds will be stronger and more beautiful if they seem to be functioning as clouds in the air, than if you make them half-rocks. Furthermore, your strong elements (the earth) will be strengthened by the proper juxtaposition of textures.

If you model your clouds with an idea of giving them a round bulk, you will find that your highlights seldom or never happen at the very edges of your form. Besides, unless the cloud is very dense, a little of the blue sky (or whatever happens to be back of your cloud) shows through the cloud at the edges, lowering the white a trifle. Look sharply at the edge on the next cloud you see, away from the sun, and the grayness of the edge (compared with the highlights) will be apparent.

Another common mistake is the tendency of beginners to paint all the clouds of the sky (small or great, dense or thin) exactly the same color and value. Try to feel that the thin, filmy fragments of clouds are much lower in value (and cooler in color) than any fat mother-cloud. These fragments are mostly torn from a larger cloud. The reason for the smaller clouds' darker value and cooler color is their semi-transparency. The blue sky, in other words, shows *through* the thinner clouds, causing the thinnest fragments to become mere filmy blue-gray against the deep blue of the sky. Note also the difference in character of these thin fragments. While a large cloud appears to be swelling up from the inside, these fragments seem to be *gouged out* by the wind, leaving stringy filaments in remnants of bluish-gray, of *concave character*. (Diagram No. 38.)

It is true of all fragments of clouds, whether torn from the main body of some larger cloud, or whether a formation or identity of their own, that the smaller the fragment or wisp is, the cooler and darker it is. Thus, from the largest wisps to the smallest, there is a graded color gamut, from warm silver-white to a cool blue-gray, with the value always lowering, as the size decreases.

Another thing to consider here, in our study of clouds, is their radial movement. On a cloudy day the clouds appear to come out of one quarter of the sky. This quarter

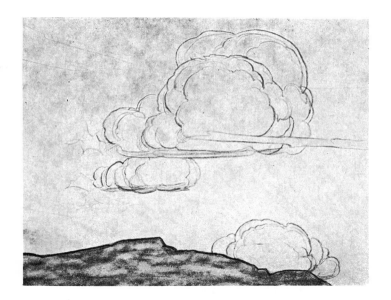

Diagram 38: Cumulus clouds. These clouds seem to expand in rounded billows from within, and maintain a complacent poise and luxurious softness.

is called the "point-of-wind" in nautical language. Exactly like the tracks in a big railroad yard, which appear to come out of a distant and small point, widening out as they approach us in well-described radii, so the clouds looming up from behind the horizon appear to grow in size and increase in speed as they sail over the firmament. The speed and quality of the wind which drives them determines their character, ranging all the way from a ragged, fragmentary, torn cloud, to the self-contained and majestic cumulus. The ability to feel this point-of-wind in an arrangement of clouds in a picture does much toward suggesting that movement without which clouds appear like painted waves—static, frozen, dead and uninteresting. An understanding of this perspective or "point" in clouds will sometimes enable you to rearrange a sky to a better "line" with the other elements in your picture, and still preserve a natural consistency.

You can decorate or "spot" your blue sky with white clouds to make a design, as you wish, but if you do not feel this other "coming-from-somewhere" quality in clouds, your sky will appear dead. Sometimes there is so little to lay hold of in a sky, to help this movement, that it becomes a difficult task. Experiment in charcoal with radially-drawn

lines to guide you in placing clouds radially, decorating your sky, but also giving the clouds a *direction.* (Diagram No. 22.) They move in absolutely parallel lines, but to our eyes seem to begin or terminate in one vanishing point beyond the horizon—just like railroad tracks.

A sky that is seen merely as a white-on-blue design or pattern loses its most sublime quality—movement; by all means get the pattern but get the motion, too. The latter requires more imagination than the former. The former is cold-blooded craft; the latter is born of feeling. Note, above all things, in what manner the wind is pushing the clouds across the firmament and what happens to the forms of the clouds themselves. Clouds have a curious consistency in character. Clouds may come and go while you are painting, but on ordinary days they will all be *doing* exactly the same things for hours at a time, in spite of their multitudinous variety of shapes. There are other days that change very rapidly meteorologically, as with sudden squalls, etc. But even these transient moods have their given character within their short careers, and if you have noted the general, you can more easily grasp the particular.

Let us consider the prime difference in

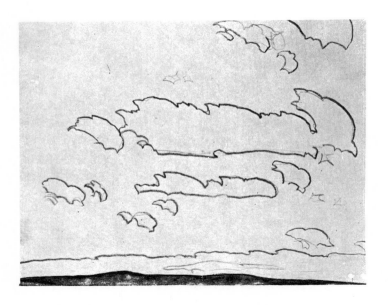

Diagram 39: Alto-cumulus clouds. The serrated tops occur because the upper air is moving with greater swiftness than the lower.

feeling between a quiet cumulus cloud hanging in the eastern sky just before sundown, and the more dramatic effects. If you watch the cumulus carefully (Diagram No. 38) you will see that it seems to expand in rounded billows from within. The hot, moist vapors of the earth are rising to it, and feeding it. There is a luxurious softness about its complacent poise—it moves but little, laterally, but seems to swell up in slow majesty with voluminous folds until the horizon is reached. This type of cloud is essentially a "fair-and-warmer" cloud, although it may afford both showers and thunder. The warm, hazy light of late after-

noon in summer seems to produce this cloud miracle. It is very rarely seen in winter, and seldom at night. Its quiet line-scheme and golden color produces a sensation of restfulness, inspires meditative thought in the beholder.

Compare this cloud with the scudding wind-racked (alto-cumulus) clouds of a winter twilight (Diagram No. 39), and you will have two extremes in form. The latter clouds occur when the upper air moves in *greater swiftness* than the lower, and the upper edges, therefore, lose the easy roll of the cumulus and become more or less serrated with dentations, *always inclined away*

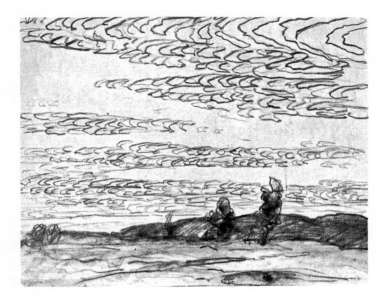

Diagram 40: Cirrus clouds. The most beautiful clouds of all, and the most difficult to paint.

Carlson's Guide to Landscape Painting

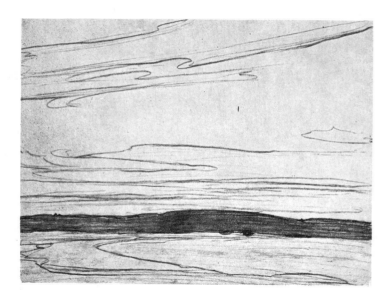

Diagram 41: Stratus clouds. Least interesting as design, these clouds are comparatively easy to paint.

from the point-of-wind, almost as if the upper part of the cloud were tumbling forward (very suggestive of accumulated motion). Such clouds are usually of cold color: dark steel-gray against a wan lemon-yellow sky. It is what fishermen call "the night-rack." An unrestful, lugubrious, and threatening gesture is projected by its line and color.

The cirrus or "mare's-tail" cloud is probably the most beautiful cloud of all. (Diagram No. 40.) I can recall but few landscapes, however, wherein they play an important part of the Scheme. (This may be because they are tremendously difficult to paint.) While each individual cloud of the cirrus variety is but a semi-circular wisp of vapor, yet these wisps are so artfully arranged by the air-currents into fantastic sweeps of *design* that they baffle description. This design ranges from heroic semicircular sweeps (called a "mackerel sky") to a wave-within-wave arabesque; sometimes this design takes on a quality that resembles the grain and knots of a silver-birch board. A consistent conformation to linear perspective in the groups and "sweeps" should be noted.

The cirrus, because of its great height and diminutive bulk, is never very white in color or light in value. The same law applies to

this as applies to "fragments." I always feel that the cirrus is a "moonlight cloud," although it appears at any time of day. In a decorative work, when an intricate design is needed to offset a necessary simplicity in other parts, the cirrus cloud is most useful. That does not imply that we must not paint a cirrus sky whenever the spirit moves us.

The stratus clouds are perhaps the least interesting as design, and they are comparatively easy to paint. (Diagram No. 41.) They conform, for the most part, to gradations of whites. When combined with cumulus, they become most beautiful. They then become a problem of "white against near-white," with infinitesimal and baffling differences of color. They possess that lazy line and gentle color that impart to the beholder a feeling of "comfort."

The nimbus or rain-cloud need not be touched upon at great length. It probably possesses a greater variety of form than all the other clouds, with their altos (half-steps). It can float at various levels and assume all shapes. It can be a luminous vapor or a low-hanging pall. In the latter instance, only its lower edges are seen, one relieved against another, ragged and torn into various patterns. While these forms conform to linear perspective (diminution in recession), they often reverse and upset the general color-and-value gradations. I mean, for instance, that a very large and dense cloud-mass overhead may assume a cold blue color in its bases, while a distant mass may assume a warm chocolate-gray in its bases. It is impossible to enumerate the possible exceptions. Expressively, the nimbus is not a very cheerful cloud. It has neither the robust threat of a windcap, nor the frank lugubriousness of the scudding night-rack. It is merely cold, damp, and insidious.

As a technical aid, in closing, I suggest that the student who begins a picture in which clouds form a part should decide at the start *where* he wants his clouds as a matter of design, and quickly proceed to draw them in, in *mass* design—and then proceed to lay in the remaining landscape to establish the big relation. He can return to the clouds later to make the necessary study of character and color. Remember, that while your clouds may have moved away, by that time others will (almost always) take their place. All will have some general character in common, for hours at a time, as you will understand through repeated observations.

A helpful method, in painting clouds, is to keep a pad or notebook at your side when starting your sketch. While laying in your general tones for your picture, keep a sharp lookout on the sky. When the clouds group themselves approximately into the "arrangement" you want for your sky, make a hasty pencil drawing of your clouds, laying stress upon their movement as well as their char-

acter. You can then paint your sky from the drawing—studying the color transitions from the clouds before you (the first clouds having by this time moved out of your vision). Make a number of "tight" drawings of clouds on differing days.

The man who does not care says "a day is a day." For the artist, there are many differences in a day, even between one time of day and another. In "poetic" terms, we have the following: the pearly or roseate morning; the waxing light of forenoon; the glare of midday; the gold of the afternoon; the descending quiet of evening, and the mystery of night.

These terms are suggestive of certain elemental truths and are based on physical fact. The morning, for instance, is never a riot of burning colors. The cause is simple: during the night the air is cooled and condensed; the sun upon rising shines through these pearly vapors and the color scheme produced is one of light airiness—pale blues, pinks, grays, silvery greens. On clear nights the dew falls heavily, and the sun rising upon dew-laden meadows is a thing to be remembered. The very heavy orange light of late afternoon that accentuates the complementary purple in the shadows is another thing entirely.

Each has its emotional potentiality. So has each hour of the day its own appeal; to the artist it is a gamut of delight. The budding landscape painter will not lose anything through quiet contemplative study of these.

II. COMPOSITION

The Expressive Properties of Line and Mass

It is certain that all lines related to rectangular or simple geometric shapes produce within us an entirely different set of emotions than do lines possessing a playfully meandering quality. Between these two extremes, there exist other lines, numerous combinations and half-steps of line that in their measure and quality react upon our feelings. Even slight knowledge of this semi-scientific truth will start us thinking.

Art is art only when it is confined within a self-imposed form. A sonata in music, an ode in poetry, a building in architecture—these become works of art through conformation to a form. All else is just noise, or babble, or a pile of stone, ends that *anybody* could achieve. Any artistic expression (a sonata, for instance) is most beautiful when it does not *obviously* follow fixed form. Thousands of sonatas have been written and thousands more will be written, all entirely different in expression, and still *sonatas.*

There are limitations to the form: its special rhythm or meter or style or color. A thing becomes a design only when invisible limitations are strictly held. Form or limitation does not *make* a work of art, but all works of art partake of a form. It requires art to speak within a given form, even if such speaking is not always art. (It is taken for granted here, of course, that the men who are going to speak within a given form are inspired men—that they have something to say with their form, and are not merely professors of form-for-its-own-sake.)

I often think that perhaps one of the reasons why Italian art was great was its conforming to a need. It was all done for a purpose, a cause, within a form. Among French examples, it is certainly this quality that makes the decorations of Puvis de Chavannes most beautiful. Remove these things from their settings or imposed limitations, and they are not quite so beautiful.

However, there is a limit even to this way of reasoning. The form I mean has not a utilitarian end, but an aesthetic beginning. The form I mean is one that should guide us in avoiding artistic pitfalls. While saying "go the limit," it also hints where that limit is, in order to save us from ranting. If we go past the limit of one aesthetic form, splashing over the edges of the comic into the tragic, for instance, we arrive at the absurd before we are aware of it.

A work of art possesses a calm dignity that waits quietly to enthrall the eye and soul. It does not scream out, nor yet hide behind cryptic or esoteric symbols. Its beauty appeals to all men, the difference is in degree. Its strength lies in the felt fountain of reserve strength, and not in breathless exhaustion.

The most expressive form or key or line-scheme or color-gamut is legitimate limitation of each attempt. Every result should be different from the last on account of the differing limitations of the form chosen for its vehicle. The choosing of expressive limitation is not child's play—it is mature choice. The painter's "vehicle" is his color, his line and mass, his form—and the pigments and materials with which he works. Having so small, and in other ways so great, a gamut from which to choose or organize his picture, intelligent selection is necessary. By all means you must choose.

A painter, like all other creators, must see through his *motif* into its significance, and then choose his *means* accordingly. It is my hope that this work will inspire in the student a habit of analysis and consideration of his artistic means, so that, when he has learned to paint, he will use the acquired craft for artistic ends. I believe that in many schools not enough emphasis is laid upon this all-important phase of art education.

I have found many students who, in "looking for something to paint," would search out the most comfortable or the shadiest spot, and there set up their easel They would, after an hour's work, be hopelessly fuddled as to why they began their sketch at all. The everyday elements in an out-of-door motif which arrest the cursory glance do so by containing something that interests us. We ought to analyze those interests and hold to them firmly. Nature, by virtue of possessing light, space, sound and movement, presents to us out of this huge storehouse an abundance of interesting and compelling images. Were we to attempt to translate more than an aesthetic impression of these wonders with our limited means (paint and canvas), we would be lost indeed. Furthermore, should we succeed, we would but reproduce a kind of secondary or imitative nature and not art, and the imitation would always suffer by contrast with the original.

Art is the transmittable, personal impression of *one quality* in the quantity before us. The other qualities possessed by the same motif we must merely use as "foils" for the main message, if we use them at all. Best of all, we can save those "other qualities" for some other canvas! It is the ability to determine consciously *what* it is that interests him, and *why,* that differentiates the artist from the art student.

Empirical knowledge comes to be a great factor in artistic creation. This is really an accumulation of experiences, and consequently accumulated emotions, transmuted in time into a general or universal emotion from which all specific emotions draw their life-blood. As an illustration, let us consider one of our inexperienced art school graduates entering the woods to sketch. A very torrent of emotion may transfix him. He stands almost aghast at the beauty of this dim-lighted green sanctuary. Feverishly he begins to paint. But soon he sadly realizes that he is unable to grasp the thing before him. He resorts to technical ruses and subterfuges; he uses every recipe or symbol he has learned. He translates it into abstract color; he translates it back again. He tries to recall all the eulogies of art he has ever read. Nothing helps.

His difficulty is that he has not visited the woods often enough to have acquired empirical knowledge or experience and the consequent accumulation of emotions. The very qualities that thrilled him upon his entrance have been dimmed in his mind by a thousand obstacles. He feels his unfitness. He goes home a sadder and a wiser man.

If he is truly wise, he will return the next day and a hundred other days. Gradually the "secret" of the woods will reveal itself to him—the tempered light and the repressed color-gamut, the preponderance of upright lines, the flickering sun-patches upon the flowery earth, the interesting "doings" of the trees, the gold-green tonality of the whole—all these things that thrilled him he will gradually recognize. He will feel and *see* his woods, by and by.

Obviously enough, a "portrait" of the woods, a mere painted snapshot, is not wanted. A snapshot is not composed of "accumulated emotions," but is a static statement of 1/100 of a second's duration. It is but one degree in the giant arc of eternity. Your picture must look like all the woods that ever grew, otherwise it is but a shell.

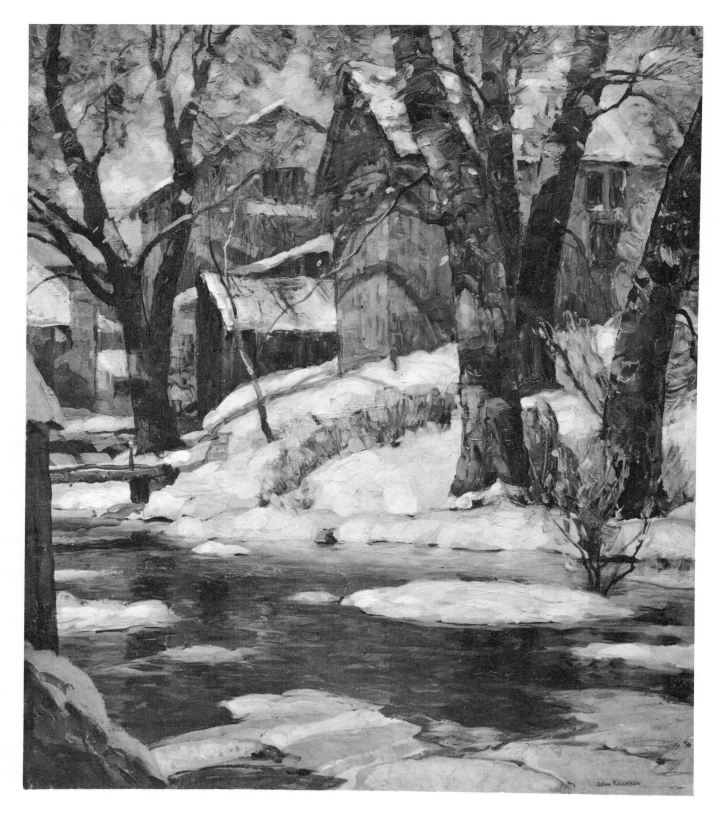

The everyday elements in an out-of-door motif which arrest the cursory glance do so by containing something which interests us.

Curiously enough, we *think* we truly appreciate long before we do. We find later we did not even *see* the things truly, because we had not yet arrived at the station that made true appreciation and consequent "vision" possible. As a result, we are forced to a gradual change of mind about things that we once thought "wonderful." Because growth is so gradual, we are correct in suspecting the virtues of anything that comes to us "overnight." If divine truths could be handed down from the old to the young, we would have arrived at omniscient perfection eons ago.

A picture may possess every attribute of good composition, decoratively speaking, and still not be significantly composed. It may be well arranged in color sequences, it may be well balanced in proportion and relation as to weights and values, it may contain an interesting variety of lines and shapes and mass, and be well modulated to its climax; it may be beautiful—it may be all these things, and yet it may not be expressive. It may be true "historically," it may be literally or physically true, and still not be a work of art. In almost every collection of pictures we find the so-called "subject pictures." They are interesting to those who consider an aggregation of sentimental, literary, or historic data as a work of art. But description belongs to the domain of letters. A work of art in paint should be beautiful and expressive as *abstract color and form* and should not interest us necessarily in any "story" outside of itself—or else it belongs to the field of illustration.

We all know this, and still each one of us lacks something of the power to do as we should like to do. Is it a lack of sensitiveness, or is it merely a lazy complacency? Or is it the fault of spontaneous painting in the much-vaunted "straight from the shoulder" style?

Too much reality in a picture is always a disappointment to the imaginative soul. We love suggestion and not hard facts. A picture should be music in form and color, with the subject-matter the vehicle. We must not imitate the externals of nature with so much fidelity that the picture fails to evoke that wonderful teasing recurrence of emotion that marks the contemplation of a work of art.

In a portrait, we wish to paint as we *remember* the face, not as it really is, line for line. The reason the line-for-line method does not give us the feeling of the person painted, is, obviously enough, that nature is a moving, changing, living thing, possessing a soul. On the other hand, a painting is a flat canvas, with concrete static shapes drawn upon it (if we are not careful).

Blessed is he who can infuse into both form and color that suggestion of life called "movement," that artifice of form and line that gives the canvas the *sensation* of life. The moderns have called it "gesture," and the term will live. I would rather call it the "transitory moment."

Try to conjure up before your imagination the face of some friend or relative. You know that face. The things that you know about that face, as you see it in your imagination, are the vital things about it. Into that face you have somehow *wished* the things you feel about the character. It would require a great deal of self-analysis to discover what those things are, but they are of paramount importance. Paint your feelings about the character, as well as the likeness.

I said that reality was always disappointing. Have you ever revisited in mature years the places of your childhood? In your memory, these places and things are wrapped in a kind of golden haze. The very trees are not real trees, but glorified impersonations of trees. A cottage is a mansion, and the meadows are eternally sparkling with rich green grass and buttercups. Better not revisit them, but let them remain in your memory with that teasing uncertainty that makes them an imaginary "work of art."

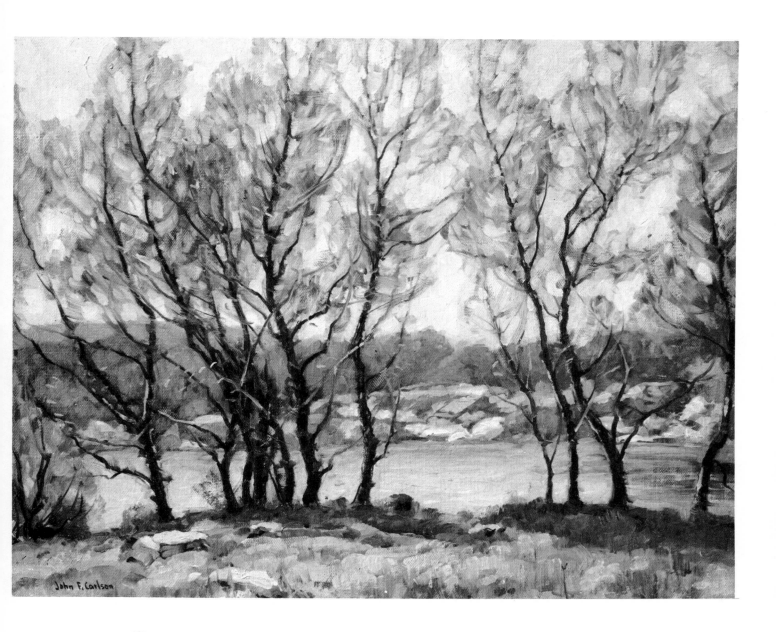

We must not imitate the externals of nature with so much fidelity that the picture fails to evoke that wonderful teasing recurrence of emotion that marks the contemplation of a work of art.

Let us consider now what tremendous possibilities exist in a stretched blank canvas before us. Let us be "intellectual" for an instant, in spite of the cry against this. Let us review our resources. We have color from light to dark, from joyous warms to gloomy cools. We have a choice of that general "color-key" for the whole canvas, that general envelope or "ensemble" without which no landscape can be a landscape, and without which it becomes a color chart. We have line and contour. Adding to this array of "means," we have the choice of general character, as well as the choice of degrees of value-contrasts. It is obvious at once that by leaning in one direction or another among the qualities given above, a tremendous expressive difference is arrived at.

The difficulty of landscape painting lies in the fact that much study is required before the student can acquire enough accumulated experience or necessary knowledge to create. The fleeting effects of light bewilder him and he has difficulty getting *anything* on his canvas. With accrued knowledge will come a sense of instinct as to just how much liberty may be taken with nature.

If a given tree, for instance, would be of more value artistically in one spot than in another in our picture, we simply *move* it to that spot—or we may leave it out entirely. If the tree or trees before us are of a character of mass or color that would impair an aesthetic completeness of our motif, we simply "transplant" other trees of more compatible character into our picture.

If we stumble upon a motif that has a tragic significance in its mass-scheme and the day otherwise has a lyric cast, we postpone painting it until a day arrives whose mood or light-effect is of a dramatic character that will *help* intensify the tragic qualities in our picture. Through understanding the emotional value of color-combinations, we may, for instance, replace a field of nodding goldenrod with a field composed of short-cropped grass and gray stones—and see how

much more dramatic or austere our picture becomes! The nodding goldenrod will be useful when we paint a breezy, sunny day, perhaps.

Of course, there are many steps between these two extreme instances of tragic and lyric, where the same goldenrod, if properly subordinated, would be of tremendous value as a color-mass, and may even be used in a dramatic picture. To illustrate this: we may be engaged upon a canvas representing a dramatic autumn day when our color gamut includes deep russets, deep rose, snappy greens and deep blue (the distant hills). In such a case the full, deep yellow of the goldenrod would help to complete the gorgeously dramatic impression.

The question arises: why *not* the yellow goldenrod in a tragic conception? The answer is that yellow is what I have termed a warm or positive color. Yellow, orange and red are positive and joyous in character. Yellow asserts itself more quickly than any other color; it "comes out" of a picture. Therefore, we try to keep what preponderances we have of yellow and its products (orange and brilliant green) in the *foreground* of our landscape. They have no place in a tragic conception. The light given by the sun gives the impression of being golden-yellow. A yellow bunch of flowers peeping in at a door or window is like a ray of sunshine, even on a dark day.

Dusky blues, deep purples, sea-greens, partake of darkness and negatives and proceed into gloom. Do not fill the foreground of your dramatic pictures with frivolous yellow and pale blue flowers. In the anxiety to get beautiful color harmony do not exhaust all combinations on one canvas, or all your canvases will be alike, and what is worse—you will accomplish nothing more significant than reproducing a manufacturer's color chart.

There is no need of a painter repeating himself with these many possibilities at hand. Every day of every season and every

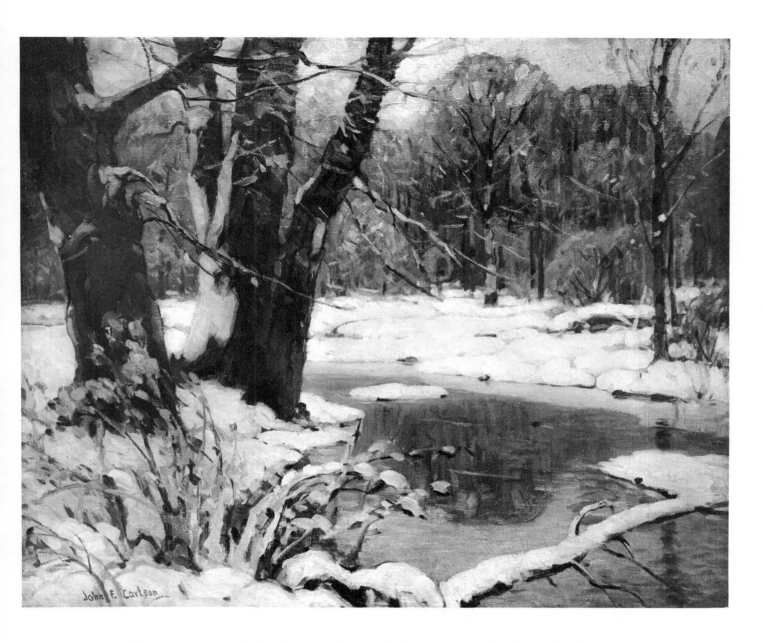

If a given tree would be of more value artistically in one spot than in another in our picture, we simply move it to that spot—or we may leave it out entirely. If the trees before us are of a character of mass or color that would impair an aesthetic completeness of our motif, we simply "transplant" other trees of more compatible character into our picture.

ten minutes of the day have their own inspiration, their own peculiar appeal, which not even the most academic, modern, or primitive conceptions can afford to disregard.

That line, mass and color, in their myriads of deviations, are the painter's true means in the abstract, is obvious to us all today. The "subject" picture, painted only for its subject and without any bearing on the aesthetics of color and line, is a thing of the past. Meissonier, Bonheur, Detaille were raconteur, naturalist and historian. They had excellent, too-excellent technique, patience, industry, and that is all. One has but to compare Detaille with Delacroix to understand why the latter makes you *feel* the battle, the other makes you see the material only. However, it is easier to criticize (especially non-constructively) than it is to draw one creative line. Were it not for a goodly amount of pure conceit inherent in each of us, we might be disturbed by the knowledge that our own work is bound to be judged by many as pure waste of time.

What rules apply to the use of the aesthetic means of line, mass and color? One cannot legislate color or composition. Men have tried it and have failed. All people react differently to different impressions, in a particular way, but very similarly in a general way.

A crowded auditorium listening to a particular piece of music reacts to it in a general way, even though there may exist great discrepancies between individual listeners as to the exact degree and shade of feeling experienced. Similarly, a certain "effect" of light, a certain unity of color contrasts or mass schemes, on any given day in the open, does not imply that several different painters, seeing this and desiring to paint it, would all paint it alike. This "effect" would and should look different to the several men, one seeing the significance of it all here, another there, in the many different qualities of the motif. They would, *one and all*, however (if the "effect" were of a lyric nature), feel the thing far removed from an austere or tragic mood. There necessarily would lie between these two a whole region of expressive possibilities to which all men would react *somewhat* similarly and yet differently —similarly in a general way, differently in a specific way.

Even the very manner of applying pigment to canvas would, in each case above, approach the lyric end, much as two different actors would *somewhat* similarly "color" their voices in taking the parts of Romeo or Macbeth, even though they might stress their own favorite lines in these roles. In painting the cherubic softness of an infant's hand against the hard harshness of the laborer's bony fist, we would all feel the contrast somewhat similarly, and yet render it differently. We are individuals, but we are still members of the same human race.

Let us now return to the proposition before us: the abstract expressive differences to be found in one kind of line and mass as against another. Just as with abstract expression or feeling, there is a tremendous difference in a line of rolling character, compared with the geometric, angular or straight line. The first is quick-moving, lively; the other inexorable, cold and profound. All lines are possible within these two extremes.

The rolling line becomes the circle, the ellipse, and the spiral. The increasing motion of a line leaving the rectilinear is caused by its degree of departure. It can be sudden; it can be gradual. (Let the student understand that the line here mentioned means the profile of contours or shapes, as well as the movement between differently related color masses.)

Upon entering a cathedral, we have all felt the awe-inspiring influence of the predominant upright or vertical lines and the right angles these effect in conjunction with the horizontal lines of the pews and floor, eased only at the vaulted height above.

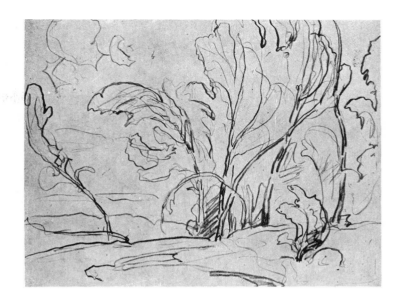

Diagram 42: The lyric or playful line.

These rectangular lines, and preeminently the *vertical* or rising lines would, I am sure, inspire a savage with awe, though he may be entirely unconscious of any religious sentiment. Add to these vertical lines, the subdued light, mellowed and enriched by the warm colors of the stained-glass windows, and you have produced a dignified, austere setting. No one, rebel or saint, escapes from the austere mood or impressions of such a setting. Similar in its quality is the feeling one has when entering the deep forest— similar line schemes and similar colors prevail; therefore similar emotions arise. Let a shaft of yellow sunlight pass into the greenish retreat and instantly the mood changes —one is tempted to sing (but one could not brook the thought of dancing the rhumba in such a wood, and certainly much less in the cathedral).

There are playful lines, ridiculous lines, grotesque lines, dramatic lines, sublime lines, tragic lines, hanging lines, aggressive lines, lethargic lines, static lines—all have their intrinsic significance. There are abstract lines that have their synonyms in musical terms; lines that correspond and are directly related to largo, andante, adagio,

prestissimo, scherzo, maestoso. There are *colors* that represent musical expression, such as apassionato, cantabile. There are lines that are related to poetic feet, to anapaest, dactyl. There are colors that are akin to poetic color, to dithyrambic or lyric poetry.

To illustrate this idea let us suppose that you had seen a lion, and had chosen to use it as your "subject matter." To merely paint a likeness of the lion would transmit nothing to the man who had not seen or read of one. The emotion that you desire to produce is not discoverable in this attitude toward your subject. Better leave alone the whiskers and the highlights of the eyes until we have decided a few of the more important propositions.

Let us try to compose or arrange our lion (with its background) so as to form the contour, weight and contrast needed for our expression of the lion, *without any of the detail*. Shall the impression be one of grandeur? Or shall it suggest the treacherous, suave, insidious, sinuous beast and its imminent lunge? Analyze your *impression* in order to approach *expression* and know that what you have created is not great

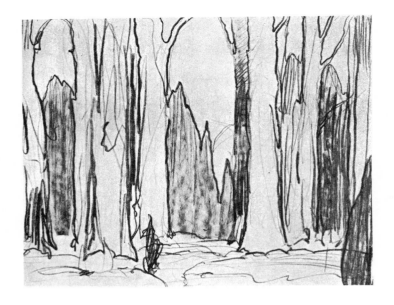

Diagram 43: The sombre upright line.

because it *suggests* a lion, but because it stirs with its beauty of conception the emotions that the lion itself made you feel.

All this is not symbolism. Symbolism is an agreement between men to let certain objects represent certain ideas, and presupposes a code. It is rather drawing upon psychological experiences (empirical with the individual and yet general to all men). In our lion picture, what is important is that even an infant must *feel* the lion. This does not mean that we can shirk the task of rendering the *likeness* of the lion well enough.

We cannot afford to let the lion look like a pig; by all means draw a "perfectly good lion," but do not stop there. Return many times to *observe* your lion; make many realistic studies as a preparation for an ultimate expressive synthesis.

The diagrams represent the difference in psychological import of the various lines and masses. We have the restful line (No. 41); the lyric or playful line (No. 42); the sombre upright line (No. 43); the tragic, disturbed line (No. 44); and the sublime or curved line (No. 45). The names

Diagram 44: The tragic disturbed line.

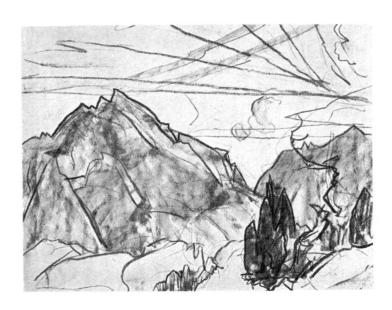

Carlson's Guide to Landscape Painting

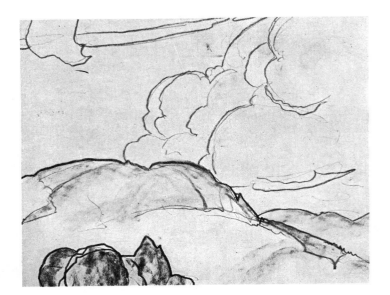

Diagram 45: The sublime or curved line.

of the lines are merely convenient handles meaning little in themselves, but the difference in their expressive qualities is everything. The diagrams show what is meant by a selection of certain dominant characteristics of mass and line scheme. Add to these an imaginary color scheme in fitness with the line scheme, and you will have gained the point I have been attempting to make in this chapter.

I suggest that the student reread the chapter on Color immediately after finishing this chapter. Many of the prime points will be found analogous. It has been a difficult task to separate color from form in so homogeneous a thing as art.

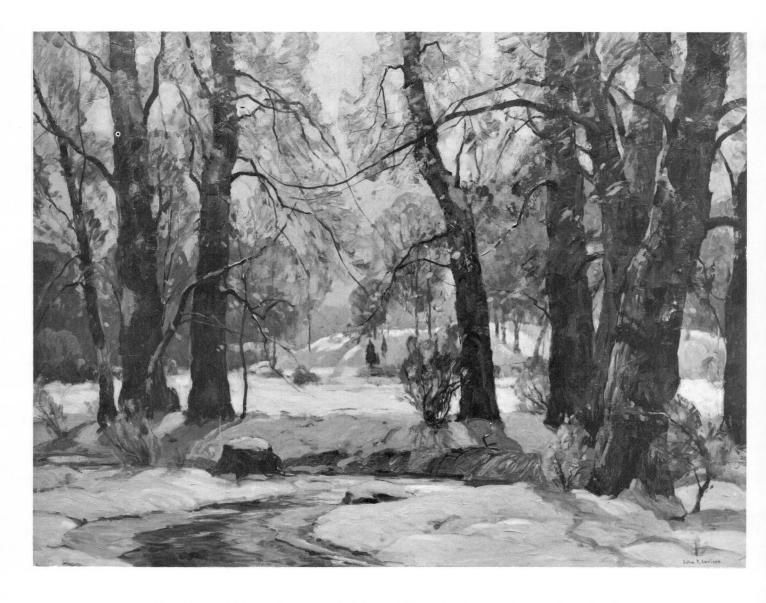

The tall upright trunks are varied in weight and value so that an irregular but interesting pattern is achieved. Note that nothing is parallel to the frame.

12. THE MAIN LINE AND THEME

While line may be a part and parcel of composition, I have found it necessary to segregate it as an abstract, pictorial department, although I realize the difficulty of such an attempt. All qualities in a work of art should merge one into another and they cannot truly be isolated for special analysis or dissection.

Yet there is something to be said for line as an abstract quality, on the one hand, as against decorative composition on the other. A canvas may be well decorated or arranged, as far as balance and spotting are concerned, and yet not possess a flow between the masses. We need masses so arranged as to form a sequence of interests in their *order of importance* in a decorative composition. (See the chapter on Design.) By "line" in a picture is here meant that quality of having a beginning, a main body, and an end.

Art is the expressive putting together of parts into a beautiful whole, and not the parts themselves. This putting together must be done not alone with the desire to create a harmony between the parts, but the parts must be arranged in their order of importance to the idea of the whole—in their proper progression or sequence. The central idea is surrounded by auxiliaries which always assist the eye to return refreshed to the central idea; and the eye escapes again into the auxiliaries for a brief instant, in order to again ascend the scale toward aesthetic thrill. This is the "line" to which we refer in this chapter.

It is impossible to give any definite rules for creating such a composition, except to give the beginner a few common sense suggestions such as: Try to keep your *most* vital and saturated color or color harmonies somewhere near the center of your design. If your arrangement of subject matter does not permit this, try to keep your most interesting or moving forms or lines near the center. (I do not here mean "center" literally, but somewhere away from the extreme edge of the picture. The eye must contemplate the picture, returning from edge to center, but at no time should it be allowed to stick at the frame.)

If you can arrange neither your most vital color nor your most interesting form near the center, try to keep your greatest contrast of dark-and-light(regardless of color) somewhere inside of your design. These suggestions may sound trite, but I have at least made you aware of the three vital means of centralizing your interest.

Where any sequence of similar or regular forms occurs, arrange the forms in such a way as to diminish in size toward the inside of your canvas rather than the reverse, thereby strengthening the suggestion of depth, or recession of space, in the canvas. (See the chapter on Linear Perspective.) If you do the reverse of this, arrange the other elements to offset it.

When detail is added to your masses, keep it suppressed in the outer masses. Do not leave it out. It is easier to centralize the interest in a composition with added *light* masses than with added *darks*. Commanding rich color or commanding forms are both pregnant means.

Arrange the lines of your prominent

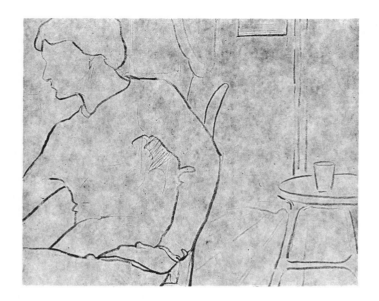

masses in such a way as to point inward toward the center of the picture. To illustrate this idea I have drawn three or four diagrams to show instances where the lines do not point inward, but outward, giving the feeling that the picture has slipped in its frame. These are illustrations of the breaking of conventional rules, a sign of exuberance and good artistic health at times. But there are certain conventions which cannot be broken in the field of arrangement. What great portrait was ever painted wherein the prime subject was placed in the very unconventional manner of Diagram No. 46?

It cannot be done, unless we so ornament and use the background space as to have the background the "portrait." Then why the sitter at all, unless as a small incidental figure? At best, such an arrangement looks like a stupid fragment of a larger composition.

In the same way, were I to break the convention of the "return" line (Diagram No. 47), I might create a beautiful color chart or a decorative arrangement of space, but not a line. This diagram has but one direction in it and we are bumped against the frame until weary.

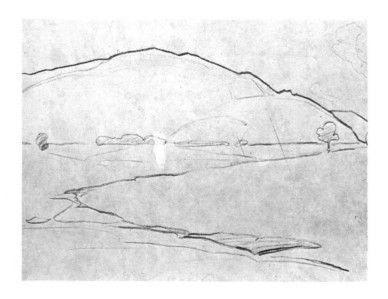

Diagram 47: The main line here has an end outside of the canvas, and the person seeing this canvas feels cheated.

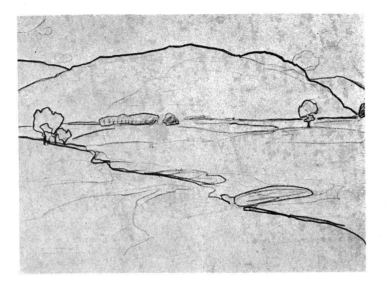

Diagram 48: Introducing a counter-line into Diagram 47 has the disastrous effect of causing the eyes to become "walled," one to each side. This also gives us too many parallel lines.

Any sensitive person seeing tnis canvas would feel he was being cheated out of something that was happening to the big lines and that they were converging outside the canvas. Perhaps a "school" will some day arise whose transitory slogan will be that of painting something *outside of the canvas."*

In Diagram No. 48 I have illustrated an attempt to stay the eye from sliding off the right edge of the canvas by the introduction of a counter-line, with the disastrous result of having the eyes become "walled," one eye to one side and one to another. This arrangement or non-arrangement also shows

the evil of having too many parallel lines in a composition. Lines one, two, three and four are practically parallels.

Let us now see a converse diagram, where all the lines point too much and too suddenly to the inside of the picture. (Diagram No. 49.) We *could* find nature arranged this way, but we would choose to rearrange her. In this diagram all lines of perspective and construction point to the cross placed in the sky. But, since *that* place is neither interesting nor beautful (it is, in fact, a piece of void blue sky, with desultory clouds), there is no reason for so arranging the material at hand. We need some other *idea* of

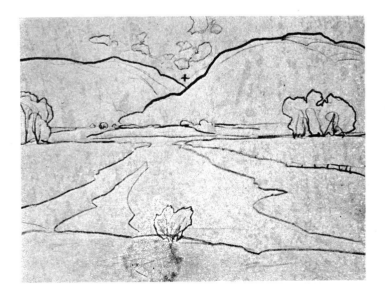

Diagram 49: All the lines here point too much and too suddenly to the inside of the picture.

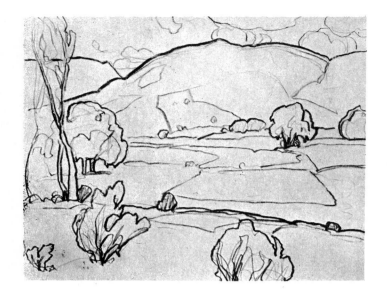

the whole picture. As it stands it is just a sketch from nature, neither lyric nor dramatic nor humorous. It is a "bread-and-butter sketch." All the elements or materials are of equal importance. It has not a good idea of space, or movement, nor is it even ornamental. Almost any change in it would benefit it. (In a *good* composition, any change is ruinous.)

Let us try one more diagram and see whether we can arrange the same materials in a more flowing and sequential manner. (Diagram No. 50.) Let us suppose that what we had seen to inspire us to paint this motif was a dramatic effect of light and shade over the mountain. Let us imagine the foreground to be in gloomy shadow with full light on the mountain and clouds. This line scheme would be consistent with this mood of nature. The lines drawn on the foreground represent anything you wish to imagine them: for instance, bare rock with patches of grass of different color and colonies of weeds and flowers. I have tried to make these shapes carry out the linear perspective of this semi-flat ground against the more vertical plane of the mountain as well as to decorate the ground with shapes *flowing* into the picture. In this composition the darker bush coming out of the immediate foreground was "needed" there, although

in the natural scene it might not have been there. Put your finger over the bush and see if the composition is not impaired.

The main line in this diagram may be said to be the one beginning in the foreground forms, picking up the gully on the left end of the mountain and dissipating itself in the peak of the mountain and cloud forms (all made too obviously apparent, for purposes of demonstration).

All pictures need not have such a strong line. In fact, in the best pictures it is *difficult to discover* just why the different forms of dark and light arrange and flow so beautifully, one into another. But they do this.

I recommend that the student make numerous rough mass drawings in charcoal (from imagination) of figures and landscapes, to develop the feeling for this rhythmic arrangement, in the abstract.

Do not be afraid that too much labor over a composition is going to kill the spontaneity. I have seen students who (under the praise of men who should have known better) became so proficient in this business of being spontaneous, that they turn out five brilliant "starts" for pictures per week, but who, after some years at this trade, were sadly outclassed by men of soberer beginnings. It requires grit to be a spontaneous finisher.

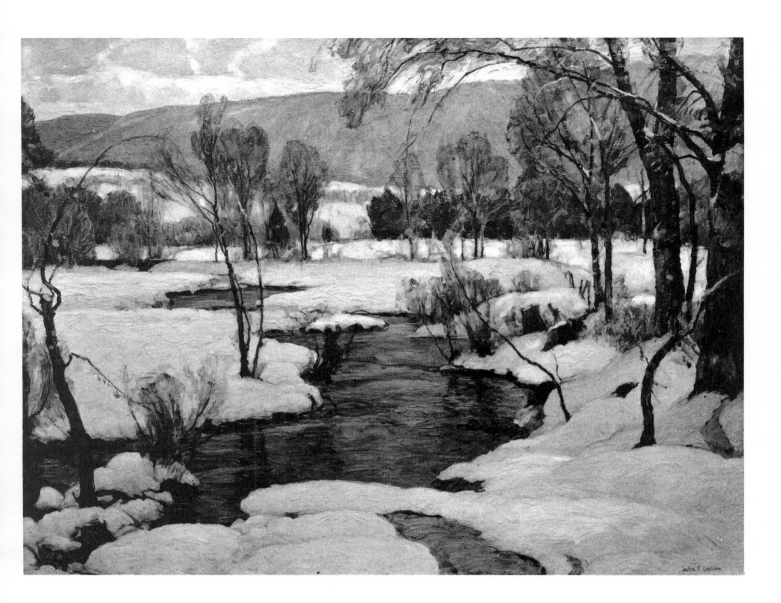

Sometimes, as in this landscape, the light comes from behind. Contrasting light and dark make a design of strong content. Do not be afraid that too much labor over the composition is going to kill the spontaneity. Those who absorb and digest their experiences are, of a sudden, mountains of strength and can produce pictures with spontaneous start *and* finish.

13. THE EXTRAORDINARY AND BIZARRE

All young painters pass through a period when they consider that a thing, in order to be "paintable," to be a proper subject or motif, must embody *extraordinary* elements of material and unusual effects of light. They think that it must be "different"— something of which it might be said: "You would never believe it, if you saw it in a painting." That this is the wrong approach need hardly be mentioned. Much time is lost by the novice who searches for something to paint that will quickly span the void that exists between his state and that of the master. This time and energy might be conserved for more fruitful consummations.

One need but look at the great pictures to discover that in these there is no straining for effect. The subjects are everyday, commonplace, but seen with an artist's eye and brain, and rendered without ostentation, technical or expressive. These homely objects and effects are made sublime in their transmutation, in the passage from the artist's brain to the canvas. The large or the general truths are convincing and great *because* they are commonplace and happen *often*. The accidental, sporadic, unusual, although of use, should not be painted just *because* they are rare. This would find an analogy in painting a man *because* he had a broken leg.

A great man can make a work of art of any objective material or inspiration he chooses, but it would be in spite of, rather than *because* of the subject matter being extraordinary.

We run 2,000 miles to see one of the "nine wonders" of the world, while right under our own eyes, perhaps in our own back yard, something transpires that is worth nine times nine wonders. I call this striving and searching after something extraordinary to paint, the "tourist's idea" of painting. Do not be a tourist-painter.

The casual tourist-landscapist will paint in Italy or Holland. If he is a Long Islander, his things will look like good old Long Island no matter where he goes! Often we have seen our "men of affairs" painted by a fine Oriental artist. The subject is apt to come out of the affair looking quite Oriental. It is right—it should be so.

The chances are that, if you stay at home and say something about your own period, life and environs, your art will be a sincere effort and your conscience clear. Paint Long Island and say more about it than any other man, and you will be a great artist. You will glorify yourself *and* Long Island. Remember that your own period will be just as picturesque to posterity as the seventeenth century is to you. If you must travel to paint, at least know that a work of art depends, not upon time nor place, but upon something that springs from the inner man. Remember, too, that all great men are the result of their time and place.

Rest assured that if you work every day at your art, using the materials nearest at hand, you will gradually discover such beauty in them that they will fill you with happiness. And if you paint these things with the deep understanding that comes of constant association, you will be an artist.

It is the artist's prerogative to reveal the beauty of common things to those less fortunate (who have difficulty in seeing it).

The fine things of this world were never accomplished by globe-trotting. All creative work is the testimony of some fine brain to the things, and thoughts, and sight, that are near at hand.

The amateur painter rushes over the globe, to Holland, to Venice. His friends demand that he come to paint their pet view in some summer resort, their "profile rocks," their "devil's kitchens," their "bridal-veil" falls, and their special sunsets. If this itinerary is followed, we see some nice sketches of this, that, and the other place, first-class illustrations for a travel book or illustrated lecture.

When an artist singles out (from the heterogenous mass of nature's material) the subject he is going to paint, he does so by virtue of an instinct of knowledge he possesses as to that subject's pliability to his artistic needs. In other words, he brings an *idea* to the motif before him (or, you might say, the motif gives him an idea what his idea is). If you approach nature without some idea, she is merciless in the way in which she piles lumber in your way.

It is the freedom in an artist's life that makes his life a responsible one. He can work, or he can loaf (if he has an income). He can paint anything he pleases, when he pleases, and in any way he pleases. He can either be a mere recorder, or a prophet of the beautiful. Other men have a root to work from. An artist has to grasp his creation from the encompassing void ("out of a clear sky"). He belongs to no large organized force in which many are doing exactly the same thing, lessening individual responsibility. He has no boss, who is bossed by a boss, who in turn is bossed by a boss, the final boss being a slave to precedent. The artist has nothing to lean on except his own feelings. He must find *his* way of saying and doing things. Precedents, except as in-

spiration, are likely to be his stumbling blocks. And yet in whatever way he may differ from other artists, in whatever way his work is new or unprecedented, or extraordinary, it must not smack of conscious artifice to brand it so.

It is this deep sincerity, this deep appreciation of the significance of things that makes one picture great among a thousand lesser ones, and causes us to feel, when we behold it, that we have thought and felt that way all our lives.

Theatricality is the antithesis of the above. It shouts and mouths and desires to be seen—an aesthetic prostitute. A good actor is never theatrical; his acting is the outcome of the emotions his part arouses in him. He is, therefore, most naturally natural. So with all works of art. Truly, an artist's life is a responsible one, and one of sustained effort. He has no interims of inactivity, but is painting even when he is playing. The husbanding of free time is one of the most difficult things; its lack of definite boundaries has been the downfall and danger of many men.

A word here about the so-called "unpaintableness" of some things. Nothing is unpaintable, except a black void. When someone has called a thing unpaintable, another man comes along and produces a thing of beauty from its qualities.

Every man can find a hundred things he would *not* want to paint for every one that inspires him. The word "unpaintable" does not mean that a thing *cannot* be painted. Anything can be painted, but whether it will become a work of art or not, *that is* the question which is entirely up to the painter.

This chapter is only concerned with warnings *not* to search for curiosities to paint, but to try rather to thoroughly study and understand the things around you. I have drawn a few diagrams to illustrate some of the curiosities that are so compellingly attractive to some beginners: things that

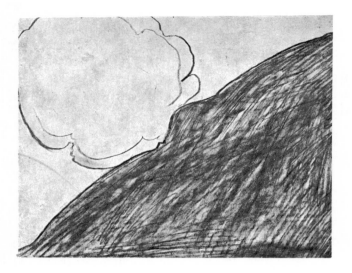

Diagram 51: A Wild Composition in which the cloud seems to fill the whole sky.

come under the same head as "Foolish Sunsets." The collection of examples might be called, in travesty, "Wild Compositions I Have Known." (See Diagrams Nos. 51, 52, 53, 54 and 55.)

Do not paint anything *because* it "looks like" something it is not, just because it has that unfortunate quality: a cloud that looks like a fish. Avoid painting the gable of a house that looks like a face, trees that appear to be "slipping off a bank," or reflections in a pool so clear "you could turn the picture upside down, and never know it." Don't paint bluebirds in a winter picture "because they stand for happiness"; nor three trees of similar size and character, "because one is red, one yellow, and one

green"; nor a series of hills, "because they look like waves." Try rather to paint a cloud that moves and feels like a cloud, and mountains that look like anything *but* waves. Later you can make these function in artistic needs.

It is admitted that any curiosity might be incorporated in a picture, if it functions as a means toward a legitimate end—that is, *not for itself*. Any object in a picture that calls too much attention to itself *as* an object, weakens the thrust of the whole idea, whether that attention is commandeered through the peculiarity, faultiness, distortion, incongruousness, or too-literal perfection of that object.

You have often heard people say of a

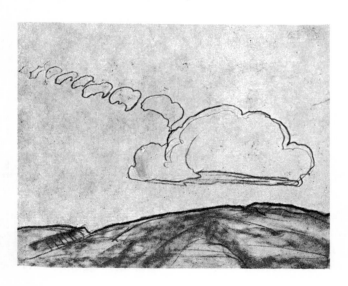

Diagram 52: A Wild Composition in which the cloud appears to move like a motor boat.

Carlson's Guide to Landscape Painting

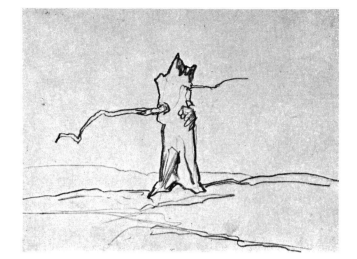

Diagram 53: A Wild Composition of a dead tree that could never have grown this way.

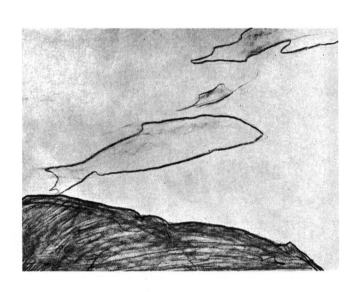

Diagram 54: A Wild Composition with a cloud that looks just like a fish.

Diagram 55: A Wild Composition of a sky that looks as if it has just cracked.

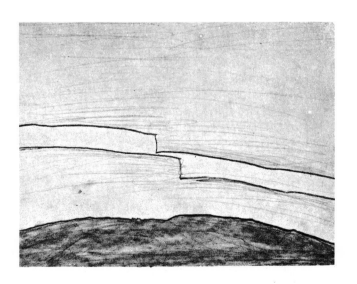

sunset: "You wouldn't believe it if you saw it painted" (and after a while you won't believe that anybody *would* paint it). There are several aesthetic reasons why a sunset *a la flamme* cannot, for its own sake, be considered expressive in a work of art. Among my reasons are the following: Red and yellow are aesthetically exciting, and seemingly fast-moving colors; to hold such a color scheme expressively would require a rampant line scheme, such as sheer and tortuous mountain silhouettes, with a rolling line scheme in the clouds, etc. Now, the most brilliantly-colored sunsets usually occur in the desert and flat lands, where atmospheric density affords prismatic refraction, and seldom in the mountains where the rarefied atmosphere contains little moisture. The flat line scheme of strata (sheet) clouds and flat horizon is artistically incompatible with the brilliance of red and yellow sunsets happening above them. Therefore, I may say that a "sunset seldom happens in the right setting."

The brilliant color-play of a sunset sky is generally out of harmony with our actual feelings concerning evening. These emotions, varying with the physical conditions of our bodies or spirits, range from a descending restfulness of well-being to an almost fearful spiritual depression. Evening is suggested by the growing darkness and mystery (descent into a minor key) or the silent flight of a bird towards its nest across a darkening woodland. Any color scheme *except* brilliant yellow-and-red would express our feelings.

The old saying about "seeing red" when we are very excited is in perfect accord with this. I can imagine a mighty battle scene, heroically silhouetted against a red and yellow sky, much better than I can against a background of peaceful meadow and brook. Sunsets are often extraordinary and unpaintable because of their natural but paradoxical colors.

Try to see nature not as a performer of pranks, but as a worthy actor of homogeneous drama, whose every variation and change is charged with worthy significance.

But also try to choose consistent settings for these. Anyone can learn to paint and to analyze physical truths as *facts,* but few have the power of self-analysis. The artist must first be a dreamer, and then a sane analyzer of those dreams. Again, "there can be no expression without previous impression."

Learn to discern the exact boundary between synthetic re-creation, suggestion, and mere caricature. In caricature lies the weakness of our so-called "modern" ideas of art. The best "modern" painters do not stoop to caricature. A form may be so modulated, so reshaped, so transmuted, that it fits perfectly into our ideas of certain requisites in a picture, *but one more step* past this line of good sense brings us to the abyss of caricature, and all is again weak and puerile; for the shapes have become extraordinary, and call our attention to their bizarreness.

Caricature is not really art; it is a travesty on art, and is very easily arrived at. Art possesses the poignance of caricature, with the reserve of profundity. A great work of art is complete. It is not the result of concentration on any *one* department. It does not "go" for *color,* or for *organization,* or for *movement,* or for symbols requiring a code. It has the best of all these things in it— hidden away, if you will. It needs no explanation, nor apology.

14. PAINTING FROM MEMORY

Enough stress cannot be laid upon the importance of memory work. Our art schools are so constituted that they seldom point out, even tentatively, the need for development along this line. Students are taught to paint what they see, and very often the pupil with the least imagination will excel in the craft and win prizes.

In landscape painting, especially, the need is great for something more than commonplace truths. *Mood* is the prime differentiating quality between a sketch and a picture. If impression is the mother of expression, then the more poignant impressions that a sensitive brain stores up, the more likelihood of some future expression. Lock an infant in a room, hold him prisoner until he is fifteen years old, and he could no more be expected to have anything to express than he could as an infant.

Storing up the impressions is not enough, however. There are men who work from morning till night with much pride, who would be better off were they strapped in a chair, and forced to *meditate* for a time.

I firmly believe that memory work, a lot of it, takes the place of such a drastic measure. A man who has learned something of the craft of painting should first contemplate a subject with the intention of rendering his impression in paint. Then he should quietly go over each mass and color relation in his mind, deciding this and that about the best way to order the whole—rehearsing his part, so to speak. Then he should turn his back upon the whole and paint from memory. He will be in a better position to say something vital about his subject than the man who must always have his "model." This does not mean that great artists do not work with their subject present. They do, but they have learned with much struggle to "memorize" in the sight of nature.

The memory exaggerates the essentials; the trifles of incidents tend to become blurred. Protracted painting of what one sees before him dulls the initial expressive shock. In painting from memory, the whole stress is laid on expressive agents. In direct-from-nature painting, much useless lumber insinuates itself, interesting for its own sake, but derogatory to the whole. The eye is greedy. There is always too much material seen, with not enough synthesis.

Until mastery of memory is reached, the brain refuses to act as the filter. I do not know how the brain exercises this function of "filtering" the mass of non-essentials heaped upon it by the eye. It is not the same thing as sensitiveness, pure and simple, for many are sensitive to impressions to a degree, and yet cannot react from the emotional experience and begin re-creating it in transmittable terms. Nor is it a "will to see" in our brain. We are continually amused or startled by the *kind* of things we do remember. Things we will to remember escape our memory and other seemingly unimportant things, sometimes pure absurdities, remain.

I am inclined to believe that all creative work is founded upon our earliest impressions, the time when the eye looked with unclouded freshness and candor upon the world! These impressions (rejecting nothing, passing judgment on nothing, accepting all), after ripening or mellowing with time into a subconscious treasure-trove, form the principal wells or founts of inspiration for the grown man. From these we select. We see something that stirs our soul with creative desire, because we recognize or remember subconsciously an old experience.

It is because of this that we may be said to paint, or write, or act what we ourselves *are* in every movement and every thought. What we are is not the result of present experience alone, but of the aggregate past. In other words, we see and feel certain things today because we have previously seen them in our most impressionable years. We add to this our present "facility" and organizing faculty, which can only be acquired in mature years. Our visions take form, gathering volume as they move, and mould themselves, sometimes sublimely, into present expression. The artist himself is often surprised at the finished work of art. He cannot tell "how it happened," nor could he repeat the feat at someone's bidding.

It is because memory revives the dormant and stimulates action, that painting from memory is here so urgently advocated. In painting, the memory will be discovered to be a very meagre thing at first. Difficulty will be found in retaining anything. But with practice the faculty will be surprisingly strengthened, not as a mere camera lens, but as a power in discerning the significant factors behind commonplace experiences.

A great deal of knowledge must be acquired through direct observation before memory can function unhampered. There would be no sense in advising the beginner to work from memory, when he is still struggling to master his *means.*

"It is the *difficulty* with which sublime things are achieved, that accounts for the rarity of them," says Spinoza. A thing that anybody could do without trying is a horrible nightmare to those creatively gifted. Fun

lies in the trying. In the trying we are learning all about means. Without knowing it, we are even developing our own particular style —one that will forever stamp us as individuals, aside from any expressive idiosyncrasies or choices we may develop.

As we progress, our work becomes more intensely absorbing. We almost live in a world apart. In memory work we relive our experiences and the effect they produced on us. We enthusiastically endeavor to put on canvas what we saw and felt, and in this way also unconsciously employ an original handling. The mind is dealing more with *expression of thought* than with the clever application of paint, and we now enter into the realm of true art.

A work is only art in the measure that it gives us the truth, translated into emotions aroused in the soul of the artist. It has been truly said that there is no work that shows so thoroughly the state of mind of the worker as painting.

Memory work is also the best method for developing the landscape sense. The Japanese are said never to draw from nature, and are shocked to see Occidentals setting their easels up before their motifs. A Japanese will make mental notes before his subject, watching every move (in the case of drawing an animal), noting the character that differentiates his animal's motion from all others. He will then go away and make a drawing from memory. If he fails in his synthesis he will return and study some more, until he arrives at a more perfect impression. This kind of impression carried into landscape painting is of vital value to the student.

In memorizing you can lean on your knowledge of the general to help you decide the particular, that is, you can note in what way and to what degree the particular thing you are contemplating differs from the ordinary. When teaching landscape classes at the Art Students' League, I often conducted groups of students to a previously selected

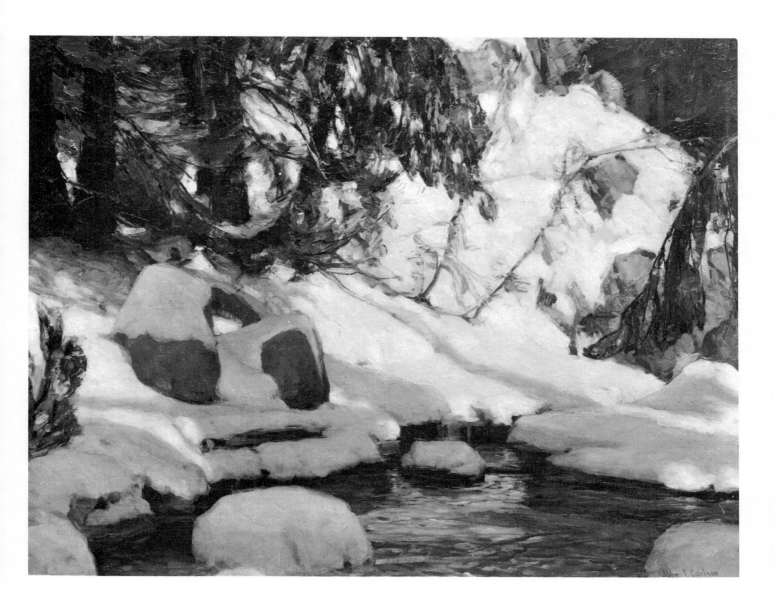

Remembering the mood makes the prime difference between a sketch and a picture. It is because memory revives the dormant and stimulates action, that painting from memory is here so urgently advocated. With practice the faculty of remembering will be surprisingly strengthened, not as a mere camera lens, but as a power in discerning the significant factors behind commonplace experiences.

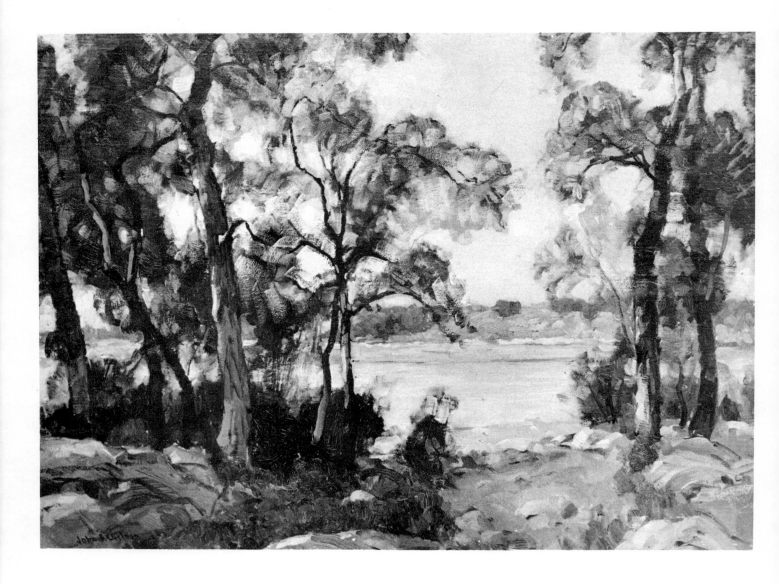

If you train yourself in memory work, you fearlessly attack and rearrange your material, for you can retain your original impression. Otherwise, you have to return continually to your motif out-of-doors, with the result that successive and different impressions may engender an ambiguous approximation in your picture.

spot, in the late afternoon or evening. The students were then supposed to paint a memory sketch the following day, embodying the qualities of the discussion of the evening before. We always began our study by taking the thing as a whole first, and then proceeding to examine each component mass and color, always bearing in mind the idea of the whole. The results were always most gratifying, not always *as* results, but as factors in stimulating the imagination of the students. The most interesting part was this: that while we had all used the same language in discussing the thing verbally, the appearance of the scene in paint later was both different and thrilling (sometimes even a bit terrifying!).

In these classes I never insisted much on construction or drawing; not even upon form, except as betrayed by color transitions or gradations. The main idea was to paint the unifying tonality, the mood, the correct placing of the masses as color in a receding plane; that is, to make things take their place in the landscape, in a desired degree of dark-and-light. The ability to place a canvas in any given key, from very dark to very light, and hold the color in purity, is a great technical asset. Sometimes changing into another key proves an artistic gain to the expression of the whole, even though

such a transposition might be termed a "cold-blooded" technical exercise.

Probably the most important by-product of memory work is the stimulation of the powers of invention. Even after you have learned to paint, your out-of-door studies or sketches are seldom the full expression of your true reaction to the beauty of your subject. The tones, and transitions, and unifying light-key may all be true and lovely; but seldom is the arrangement of these the best you can make. So many things again have intruded themselves upon your vision (and found their way to the canvas) that the more profound thing—expressive arrangement—has been cheated out of your attention. Often a complete reordering of the essentials becomes necessary.

If you have trained yourself in memory work, however, you fearlessly attack and rearrange your delinquent material, for you can retain your original impression. If not, you have to return, time and again, to your motif out-of-doors, with the result that the successive (and different) impressions gained engender an ambiguous approximation in your picture. Painting from memory, then, aids rearrangement, and rearrangement is the mother of pure invention. Convention is craft; invention is art. In art, knowledge assists invention.

INDEX

Carlson's Guide to Landscape Painting